W9-CLG-967

Modern Critical Interpretations

Henry David Thoreau's
Walden

Modern Critical Interpretations

These and other titles in preparation

Modern Critical Interpretations

Henry David Thoreau's
Walden

Edited and with an introduction by

Harold Bloom
Sterling Professor of the Humanities
Yale University

Chelsea House Publishers
NEW YORK ◇ PHILADELPHIA

TECHNICAL COLLEGE OF THE LOWCOUNTRY
LEARNING RESOURCES CENTER
P. O. BOX 1288 026811
100 S. RIBAUT ROAD
BEAUFORT, S. C. 29901

27.95

4-9-91

© 1987 by Chelsea House Publishers, a division
of Main Line Book Co.

Introduction © 1987 by Harold Bloom

All rights reserved. No part of this publication may be
reproduced or transmitted in any form or by any means
without the written permission of the publisher.

Printed and bound in the United States of America

10 9 8 7 6 5 4 3 2

∞ The paper used in this publication meets the minimum
requirements of the American National Standard for
Permanence of Paper for Printed Library Materials,
Z39.48-1984.

Library of Congress Cataloging-in-Publication Data
Thoreau's Walden.
    (Modern critical interpretations)
    Bibliography: p.
    Includes index.
    Summary: A collection of eight critical essays on Thoreau's
"Walden" arranged in chronological order of publication.
    1. Thoreau, Henry David, 1817–1862. Walden. [1. Thoreau,
Henry David, 1817–1862. Walden. 2. American literature—
History and criticism] I. Bloom, Harold. II. Series.
PS3048.T48 1987   818'.303   87-9306
ISBN 1-55546-012-7

Contents

Editor's Note

This book gathers together a representative selection of the best criticism of Thoreau's *Walden* published since Stanley Cavell's *The Senses of Walden* (1972) which can be said to be the prelude to our contemporary reading of Thoreau's masterwork. The critical essays are reprinted here in the chronological order of their original publication. I am grateful to Peter Childers for his aid in editing this volume.

My introduction constitutes a minority report upon Thoreau and upon *Walden* and emphasizes the anxiety of influence induced in the disciple by his master, Emerson. The chronological sequence begins with two celebrations of Thoreau the naturalist. Loren Eiseley finds in *Walden* instruction for all of us, since we have fallen out of nature, while George Sibley returns to the woods to read *Walden* in its proper context.

The economic metaphor crucial to *Walden* (a metaphor original with Emerson) is redefined by Judith P. Saunders as Thoreau's quest never to pay more for a thing than it is worth. Harold Hellenbrand, in the wake of Cavell, also praises *Walden*'s "organic economy" as a triumph of sublimation. From a different perspective, Ronald B. Shwartz views *Walden* as an essentially private discourse that does not break out of Thoreau's intense solipsism.

In an examination of writing, genealogy, and history in *Walden*, Joseph G. Kronick finds another American instance of our literature proving "less a beginning than a continual destruction of the old." Handling the metaphor of economics in a way rather different from Thoreau's own, Michael T. Gilmore shows that "far from impairing the quality of *Walden*, commercial considerations conspired to make it a better work."

Robert Weisbuch fittingly concludes this volume with an account of how *Walden* evades and transcends the influence upon it of Wordsworth and Coleridge. My introduction, with its doubts as to whether Thoreau could evade and transcend Emerson, should provide a useful contrast to Weisbuch's more generous estimate of *Walden*.

Introduction

I

All of us, however idiosyncratic, begin by living in a generation that over-determines more of our stances and judgments than we can hope to know, until we are far along in the revisionary processes that can bring us to a Second Birth. I myself read *Walden* while I was very young, and "Civil Disobedience" and "Life without Principle" soon afterwards. But I read little or no Emerson until I was an undergraduate, and achieved only a limited awareness of him then. I began to read Emerson obsessively just before the middle of the journey, when in crisis, and have never stopped reading him since. More even than Freud, Emerson helped change my mind about most things, in life and in literature, myself included. Going back to Thoreau, when one has been steeped in Emerson for more than twenty years, is a curious experience. A distinguished American philosopher, my contemporary, has written that he underwent the reverse process, coming to Emerson only after a profound knowing of Thoreau, and has confessed that Emerson seemed to him at first a "second-rate Thoreau." I am not tempted to call Thoreau a second-rate Emerson, because Thoreau, at his rare best, was a strong writer, and revised Emerson with passion and with cunning. But Emerson was for Thoreau even more massively what he was for Walt Whitman and all Americans of sensibility ever since: the metaphor of "the father," the pragmatic image of the ego ideal, the inescapable pre-cursor, the literary hero, the mind of the United States of America.

My own literary generation had to recover Emerson, because we came after the critics formed by the example and ideology of T. S. Eliot, who had proclaimed that "the essays of Emerson are already an encumbrance." I can recall conversations about Emerson with R. P. Blackmur, who in-formed me that Emerson was of no relevance, except insofar as he repre-sented an extreme example for America of the unsupported and catastrophic

1

Protestant sensibility, which had ruined the Latin culture of Europe. Allen Tate more succinctly told me that Emerson simply was the devil, a judgment amplified in my single conversation with the vigorous Yvor Winters. In many years of friendship with Robert Penn Warren, my only disputes with that great poet have concerned Emerson, upon whom Warren remains superbly obdurate. As these were the critical minds that dominated American letters from 1945 to 1965 (except for Lionel Trilling, who was silent on Emerson), it is no surprise that Emerson vanished in that era. From 1965 through the present, Emerson has returned, as he always must and will, because he is the pragmatic origin of our literary culture. Walt Whitman and Emily Dickinson, Robert Frost and Wallace Stevens, Hart Crane, Elizabeth Bishop and John Ashbery have written the poems of our climate, but Emerson was and is that climate.

How does Thoreau now read in our recovered sense of the Emersonian climate? Is the question itself unfair? Rereading *Walden* and the major essays, I confess to an experience different in degree, but not in kind, from a fresh encounter with Thoreau's verse. As a poet, Thoreau is in the shadow of Wordsworth, towards whom his apotropaic gestures are sadly weak. In prose, conceptually and rhetorically, Thoreau strongly seeks to evade Emerson, wherever he cannot revise him directly. But this endless agon, unlike Whitman's, or the subtler subversion of Emerson by Dickinson and by Henry James, is won by the image of the father. Rereading Thoreau, either I hear Emerson overtly, or more darkly I detect him in what Stevens called "the hum of thoughts evaded in the mind."

II

During that 1945–1965 heyday of what then was called "the New Criticism," only *Walden,* among all of Thoreau's works, was exempt from censure. I have never understood the New Critical tolerance for *Walden,* except as a grudging bit of cultural patriotism, or perhaps as a kind of ultimate act of revenge against Emerson, the prophet who organized support for John Brown, cast out Daniel Webster because of the Fugitive Slave Act, and burned himself into a premature senility by his fierce contempt for the South and its culture throughout the Civil War. Thoreau, no less an enthusiast for John Brown, and equally apocalyptic against the South, somehow escaped the wrath of Tate, Warren, and their cohorts. This may have something to do with the myth of Thoreau as a kind of American Mahatma Gandhi, a Tolstoyan hermit practicing native arts and crafts out in the woods. Homespun and reputedly naive, such a fellow may have seemed harmless enough, unlike the slyly wicked Sage of Concord, Ralph Waldo Lucifer, impediment to the United States somehow acquiring a Southern and Latin culture.

The merely actual Thoreau has been so prettified that one does best to begin a consideration of the man with the opening paragraphs of Leon Edel's pungent pamphlet, in which an amiable disenchantment with our American Narcissus is memorably expressed:

> Of the creative spirits that flourished in Concord, Massachusetts, during the middle of the nineteenth century, it might be said that Hawthorne loved men but felt estranged from them, Emerson loved ideas more than men, and Thoreau loved himself. Less of an artist than Hawthorne, less of a thinker than Emerson, Thoreau made of his life a sylvan legend, that of man alone, in communion with nature. He was a strange presence in American letters—we have so few of them—an eccentric. The English tend to tolerate their eccentrics to the enrichment of their national life. In America, where democracy and conformity are often confused, the nonconforming Thoreau was frowned upon, and for good reason. He had a disagreeable and often bellicose nature. He lacked geniality. And then he had once set fire to the Concord woods—a curious episode, too lightly dismissed in the Thoreau biographies. He was, in the fullest sense of the word, a "curmudgeon," and literary history has never sufficiently studied the difficulties his neighbors had in adjusting themselves to certain of his childish ways. But in other ways he was a man of genius—even if it was a "crooked genius" as he himself acknowledged.
>
> A memorable picture has been left by Hawthorne's daughter of the three famous men of Concord skating one winter's afternoon on the river. Hawthorne, wrapped in his cloak, "moved like a self-impelled Greek statue, stately and grave," as one might expect of the future author of *The Marble Faun*. Emerson, stoop-shouldered, "evidently too weary to hold himself erect," pitched forward, "half lying on the air." Thoreau, genuinely skillful on his skates, performed "dithyrambic dances and Bacchic leaps," enchanted with himself. Their manner of skating was in accord with their personalities and temperaments.
>
> Behind a mask of self-exaltation Thoreau performed as before a mirror—and first of all for his own edification. He was a fragile Narcissus embodied in a homely New Englander. His life was

brief. He was born in 1817, in Concord; he lived in Concord, and he died in Concord in 1862 shortly after the guns had spoken at Fort Sumter. A child of the romantic era, he tried a number of times to venture forth into the world. He went to Maine, to Staten Island, to Cape Cod, and ultimately to Minnesota, in search of health, but he always circled back to the Thoreau family house in Concord and to the presence of a domineering and loquacious mother. No other man with such wide-ranging thoughts and a soaring mind—it reached to ancient Greece, to the Ganges, to the deepest roots of England and the Continent— bound himself to so small a strip of ground. "He was worse than provincial," the cosmopolitan Henry James remarked, "he was parochial."

Edel's Jamesian slight can be dismissed, since Edel is James's devoted biographer, but the rest of this seems charmingly accurate. The great con-servationist who set fire to the Concord woods; the epitome of Emersonian Self-Reliance who sneaked back from Walden in the evening to be fed dinner by Lidian Emerson; the man in whom Walt Whitman (whom Thoreau admired greatly, as man and as poet) found "a morbid dislike of human-ity"—that, alas, was the empirical Thoreau, as contrasted to the ontological self of Thoreau. Since, to this day, Thoreau's self-mystifications continue to mystify nearly all of Thoreau's scholars, I find myself agreeing with Edel's judgment that the best discussions of Thoreau continue to be those of Emerson, James Russell Lowell, and Robert Louis Stevenson. Magnif-icent (and subtly balanced) as Emerson's funeral eulogy is, and brilliant as Lowell's much-derided essay continues to be, the best single remark on Thoreau remains Stevenson's: "It was not inappropriate, surely, that he had such close relations with the fish."

Lowell, sympathetic enough to Emerson, had little imagination to countenance the even more extreme disciple, Thoreau:

This notion of an absolute originality, as if one could have a patent-right in it, is an absurdity. A man cannot escape in thought, any more than he can in language, from the past and the present. As no one ever invents a word, and yet language somehow grows by general contribution and necessity, so it is with thought. Mr. Thoreau seems to me to insist in public on going back to flint and steel, when there is a match-box in his pocket which he knows very well how to use at a pinch. Orig-inality consists in power of digesting and assimilating thoughts, so that they become part of our life and substance. Montaigne, for example, is one of the most original of authors, though he helped himself to ideas in every direction. But they turn to blood and coloring in his style, and give a freshness of complexion that is forever charming. In Thoreau much seems yet to be foreign and unassimilated, showing itself in symptoms of indigestion. A preacher-up of Nature, we now and then detect under the surly and stoic garb something of the sophist and the sentimentalizer. I am far from implying that this was conscious on his part. But it is much easier for a man to impose on himself when he measures only with himself. A greater familiarity with ordinary men would have done Thoreau good, by showing him how many fine qualities are common to the race. The radical vice of his theory of life was that he confounded physical with spiritual remoteness from men. A man is far enough withdrawn from his fellows if he keep himself clear of their weaknesses. He is not so truly withdrawn as exiled, if he refuse to share their strength. "Solitude," says Cowley, "can be well fitted and set right but upon a very few persons. They must have enough knowledge of the world to see the vanity of it, and enough virtue to despise all vanity." It is a morbid self-consciousness that pronounces the world of men empty and worthless before trying it, the instinctive evasion of one who is sensible of some innate weakness, and retorts the accusation of it before any has made it but himself. To a healthy mind, the world is a constant challenge of opportunity. Mr. Thoreau had not a healthy mind, or he would not have been so fond of prescribing. His whole life was a search for the doctor. The old mystics had a wiser sense of what the world was worth. They ordained a severe apprenticeship to law, and even ceremonial, in order to the gaining of freedom and mastery over these. Seven years of service for Rachel were to be rewarded at last with Leah. Seven other years of faithfulness with her were to win them at last the true bride of their souls. Active Life was with them the only path to the Contemplative.

It is curious that Lowell should have directed this attack upon Emersonian Self-Reliance at the disciple, not the master, yet Lowell, as he shows abundantly in his fine essay "Emerson the Lecturer," was overcome by the great lecturer's charisma, his mysterious but nearly universally acknowledged personal charm. Even Lowell's argument against Transcendentalist "solitude" would have been better directed against the author of *Society and Solitude* than the recalcitrant author of *Walden*. Lowell's essay survives, despite its unfairness, because of its accuracy, and even because of its ultimate judgment of Thoreau.

> We have said that his range was narrow, but to be a master is to be a master. He had caught his English at its living source, among the poets and prose-writers of its best days; his literature was extensive and recondite; his quotations are always nuggets of the purest ore: there are sentences of his as perfect as anything in the language, and thoughts as clearly crystallized; his metaphors and images are always fresh from the soil; he had watched Nature like a detective who is to go upon the stand; as we read him, it seems as if all-out-of-doors had kept a diary and become its own Montaigne.

To be the Montaigne of all-out-of-doors ought to have been distinction enough for anyone, yet Emerson confessed that he had hoped for more from this rugged and difficult disciple:

> His virtues, of course, sometimes ran into extremes. It was easy to trace to the inexorable demand on all for exact truth that austerity which made this willing hermit more solitary even than he wished. Himself of a perfect probity, he required not less of others. He had a disgust at crime, and no worldly success would cover it. He detected paltering as readily in dignified and prosperous persons as in beggars, and with equal scorn. Such dangerous frankness was in his dealing that his admirers called him "that terrible Thoreau," as if he spoke when silent, and was still present when he had departed. I think the severity of his ideal interfered to deprive him of a healthy sufficiency of human society.
>
> The habit of a realist to find things the reverse of their appearance inclined him to put every statement in a paradox. A certain habit of antagonism defaced his earlier writings,—a trick of rhetoric not quite outgrown in his later, of substituting for the obvious word and thought its diametrical opposite. He praised wild mountains and winter forests for their domestic air, in snow and ice he would find sultriness, and commended the wilderness for resembling Rome and Paris. "It was so dry, that you might call it wet."

The tendency to magnify the moment, to read all the laws of Nature in the one object or one combination under your eye, is of course comic to those who do not share the philosopher's perception of identity. To him there was no such thing as size. The pond was a small ocean; the Atlantic, a large Walden Pond. He referred every minute fact to cosmical laws. Though he meant to be just, he seemed haunted by a certain chronic assumption that the science of the day pretended completeness, and he had just found out that the *savans* had neglected to discriminate a particular botanical variety, had failed to describe the seeds or count the sepals. "That is to say," we replied, "the blockheads were not born in Concord; but who said they were? It was their unspeakable misfortune to be born in London, or Paris, or Rome; but, poor fellows, they did what they could, considering that they never saw Bateman's Pond, or Nine-Acre Corner, or Becky Stow's Swamp; besides, what were you sent into the world for, but to add this observation?"

Had his genius been only contemplative, he had been fitted to his life, but with his energy and practical ability he seemed born for great enterprise and for command; and I so much regret the loss of his rare powers of action, that I cannot help counting it a fault in him that he had no ambition. Wanting this, instead of engineering for all America, he was the captain of a huckleberry-party. Pounding beans is good to the end of pounding empires one of these days; but if, at the end of years, it is still only beans!

Emerson's ironies are as beautiful here as anywhere, and their dialectical undersong is wholly in Thoreau's favor. Henry Ford, a fervent and overt Emersonian, engineered for all America; and clearly Emerson himself, like many among us, would have preferred Thoreau to Ford, and a huckleberry-party to a car factory.

III

Thoreau's crucial swerve away from Emerson was to treat natural objects as books, and books as chunks of nature, thus evading all literary tradition, Emerson's writings not excepted. Unfortunately, Thoreau was not really an oppositional or dialectical thinker, like Emerson, though certain an oppositional personality, as the sane and sacred Emerson was not. Being also something of a prig and an elitist, again unlike Emerson, Thoreau could not always manage Emerson's insouciant *praxis* of building up a kind of Longinian discourse by quoting amply without citation. Self-consciousness kept breaking in, as it rarely does with Emerson, unless Emerson wills it thus. But, if you cannot achieve freedom in quotation, if you cannot convert the riches of others to your own use without a darkening of consciousness, then what can it mean to demand that books and natural objects interchange their attributes? *Walden,* for all its incessant power, is frequently uneasy because of an unspoken presence, or a perpetual absence that might as well be a presence, and that emerges in Thoreau's Journal:

> Emerson does not consider things in respect to their essential utility, but an important partial and relative one, as works of art perhaps. His probes pass one side of their center of gravity. His exaggeration is of a part, not of the whole.

This is, of course, to find the fault that is not there, and qualifies only as a weak misreading of Emerson. Indeed, it is to attribute to Emerson what is actually Thoreau's revision of Emerson, since it is Thoreau who considers things as books, not Emerson, for whom a fact was an epiphany of God, God being merely what was oldest in oneself, that which went back before the Creation-Fall. Emerson, like the considerably less genial Carlyle, was a kind of Gnostic, but the rebel Thoreau remained a Wordsworthian, reading nature for evidences of a continuity in the ontological self that nature simply could not provide.

Thoreau on "Reading" in *Walden* is therefore chargeable with a certain bad faith, as here in a meditation where Emerson, the Plato of Concord, is not less than everywhere, present by absence, and perhaps even more absent by repressed presence:

> I aspire to be acquainted with wiser men than this our Concord soil has produced, whose names are hardly known here. Or shall I hear the name of Plato and never read his book? As if Plato were my townsman and I never saw him,—my next neighbor and I never heard him speak or attended to the wisdom of his words. But how actually is it? His Dialogues, which contain what was immortal in him, lie on the next shelf, and yet I never read them. We are under-bred and low-lived and illiterate; and in this respect I confess I do not make any very broad distinction between the illiterateness of my townsman who cannot read at all, and the illiterateness of him who has learned to read only what is for children and feeble intellects. We should be as good

as the worthies of antiquity, but partly by first knowing how good they were. We are a race of tit-men, and soar but little higher in our intellectual flights than the columns of the daily paper.

It is not all books that are as dull as their readers. There are probably words addressed to our condition exactly, which, if we could really hear and understand, would be more salutary than the morning or the spring to our lives, and possibly put a new aspect on the face of things for us. How many a man has dated a new era in his life from the reading of a book. The book exists for us perchance which will explain our miracles and reveal new ones. The at present unutterable things we may find somewhere uttered. These same questions that disturb and puzzle and confound us have in their turn occurred to all the wise men; not one has been omitted; and each has answered them, according to his ability, by his words and his life. Moreover, with wisdom we shall learn liberality. The solitary hired man on a farm in the outskirts of Concord, who has had his second birth and peculiar religious experience, and is driven as he believes into silent gravity and exclusiveness by his faith, may think it is not true; but Zoroaster, thousands of years ago, travelled the same road and had the same experience; but he, being wise, knew it to be universal, and treated his neighbors accordingly, and is even said to have invented and established worship among men. Let him humbly commune with Zoroaster then, and, through the liberalizing influence of all the worthies, with Jesus Christ himself, and let "our church" go by the board.

The wisest man our Concord soil has produced need not be named, particularly since he vied only with Thoreau as a devoted reader of Plato. The second paragraph I have quoted rewrites the "Divinity School Address," but with the characteristic Thoreauvian swerve towards the authority of books, rather than away from them in the Emersonian manner. The reader or student, according to Emerson, is to consider herself or himself the text, and all received texts only as commentaries upon the scholar of one candle, as the title-essay of *Society and Solitude* prophesies Wallace Stevens in naming that single one for whom all books are written. It may be the greatest literary sorrow of Thoreau that he could assert his independence from Emerson only by falling back upon the authority of texts, however recondite or far from the normative the text might be.

One can read Thoreau's continued bondage in *Walden*'s greatest triumph, its preternaturally eloquent "Conclusion":

> The life in us is like the water in the river. It may rise this year higher than man has ever known it, and flood the parched uplands; even this may be the eventful year, which will drown out all our muskrats. It was not always dry land where we dwell. I see far inland the banks which the stream anciently washed, before science began to record its freshets. Every one has heard the story which has gone the rounds of New England, of a strong and beautiful bug which came out of the dry leaf of an old table of apple-tree wood, which had stood in a farmer's kitchen for sixty years, first in Connecticut, and afterwards in Massachusetts,—from an egg deposited in the living tree many years earlier still, as appeared by counting the annual layers beyond it; which was heard gnawing out for several weeks, hatched perchance by the heat of an urn. Who does not feel his faith in a resurrection and immortality strengthened by hearing of this? Who knows what beautiful and winged life, whose egg has been buried for ages under many concentric layers of woodenness in the dead dry life of society, deposited at first in the alburnum of the green and living tree, which has been gradually converted into the semblance of its well-seasoned tomb,—heard perchance gnawing out now for years by the astonished family. of man, as they sat round the festive board,—may unexpectedly come forth from amidst society's most trivial and handselled furniture, to enjoy its perfect summer life at last!
>
> I do not say that John or Jonathan will realize all this; but such is the character of that morrow which mere lapse of time can never make to dawn. The light which puts out our eyes is darkness to us. Only that day dawns to which we are awake. There is more day to dawn. The sun is but a morning star.

The first of these paragraphs echoes, perhaps unknowingly, several crucial metaphors in the opening pages of Emerson's strongest single essay, "Experience," but more emphatically Thoreau subverts Emerson's emphasis upon a Transcendental impulse that cannot be repressed, even if one sets out deliberately to perform the experiment of "Experience," which is to follow empirical principles until they land one in an intolerable, more than skeptical, even nihilistic entrapment. Emerson, already more-than-Nietzschean in "Experience," is repudiated in and by the desperately energetic, indeed apocalyptic Transcendentalism of the end of *Walden,* an end that refuses Emersonian (and Nietzschean) dialectical irony. But the beautiful, brief final paragraph of *Walden* brings back Emerson anyway, with an unmistakable if doubtless involuntary allusion to the rhapsodic conclusion of *Nature,* where however the attentive reader always will hear (or overhear) some acute Emersonian ironies. "Try to live as though it were morning" was Nietzsche's great admonition to us, if we were to become Overmen, free of the superego. Nietzsche was never more Emersonian than in this, as he well knew. But when Thoreau eloquently cries out: "The sun is but a morning star," he is not echoing but trying to controvert Emerson's sardonic observation that you don't get a candle in order to see the sun rise. There may indeed be a sun beyond the sun, as Blake, D. H. Lawrence, and other heroic vitalists have insisted, but Thoreau was too canny, perhaps too New England, to be a vitalist. *Walden* rings out mightily as it ends, but it peals another man's music, a man whom Thoreau could neither accept nor forget.

Walden: Thoreau's Unfinished Business

Loren Eiseley

The life of Henry David Thoreau has been thoroughly explored for almost a century by critics and biographers, yet the mystery of this untraveled man who read travel literature has nowhere been better expressed than by his own old walking companion Ellery Channing, who once wrote: "I have never been able to understand what he meant by his life. Why was he so disappointed with everybody else? Why was he so interested in the river and the woods . . . ? Something peculiar here I judge."

If Channing, his personal friend, was mystified, it is only to be expected that as Thoreau's literary stature has grown, the ever-present enigma of his life and thought has grown with it. Wright Morris, the distinguished novelist and critic, has asked, almost savagely, the same question in another form. Putting Channing's question in a less personal but more formidable and timeless literary context he ventures, quoting from Thoreau who spent two years upon the Walden experiment and then abandoned it, "If we are alive let us go about our business." "But," counters Morris brutally "what business?" Thoreau fails to inform us. In the words of Morris, Walden was the opening chapter of a life, one that enthralls us, but with the remaining chapters missing.

For more than a decade after *Walden* was composed, Thoreau continued his intensive exploration of Concord, its inhabitants and its fields, but upon the "business" for which he left Walden he is oddly cryptic. Once, it is true, he muses in his journal that "the utmost possible novelty would be

From *The Star Thrower.* © 1978 by the Estate of Loren C. Eiseley, Mabel L. Eiseley, Executrix. Harcourt Brace Jovanovich, 1978.

13

the difference between me and myself a year ago." He must then have been about some business, even though the perceptive critic Morris felt he had already performed it and was at loose ends and groping. The truth is that the critic, in a timeless sense, can be right and in another way wrong, for looking is in itself the business of art.

In a studied paragraph Carl Jung, with no reference to Thoreau, perhaps pierced closest to Thoreau's purpose without ever revealing it. He says in his alchemical studies, "Medieval alchemy prepared the greatest attack on the divine order of the universe which mankind has ever dared. Alchemy is the dawn of the age of natural sciences which, through the *daemonium* of the scientific spirit, drove nature and her forces into the service of mankind to a hitherto unheard of degree. . . . Technics and science have indeed conquered the world, but whether the soul has gained thereby is another matter."

Thoreau was indeed a spiritual wanderer through the deserts of the modern world. Almost by instinct he rejected that beginning wave of industrialism which was later to so entrance his century. He also rejected the peace he had found on the shores of Walden Pond, the alternate glazing and reflection of that great natural eye which impartially received the seasons. It was, in the end, too great for his endurance, too timeless. He was a restless pacer of fields, a reader who, in spite of occasional invective directed against those who presumed to neglect their homes for far places, nevertheless was apt with allusions drawn from travel literature, and quick to discern in man uncharted spaces.

"Few adults," once remarked Emerson, Thoreau's one-time mentor and friend, "can see nature." Thoreau was one of those who could. Moreover he saw nature as another civilization, a thing of vaster laws and vagaries than that encompassed by the human mind. When he visited the Maine woods he felt its wind upon him like the closing of a dank door from some forgotten cellar of the past.

Was it some curious midnight impulse to investigate such matters that led Thoreau to abandon the sunny hut at Walden for "other business"? Even at Walden he had heard, at midnight, the insistent fox, the "rudimental man," barking beyond his lighted window in the forest. The universe was in motion, nothing was fixed. Nature was "a prairie for outlaws," violent, unpredictable. Alone in the environs of Walden Thoreau wandered in the midst of that greater civilization he had discovered as surely as some monstrous edifice come suddenly upon in the Mayan jungles. He never exclaimed about the Indian trail seen just at dusk in a winter snowfall—neither where they went, nor upon what prairie they vanished or in what direction.

He never ventured to tell us, but he was one of those great artist-scientists who could pursue the future through its past. This is why he lives today in the heart of young and old alike, "a man of surfaces," one critic has said, but such surfaces—the arrowhead, the acorn, the oak leaf, the indestructible thought-print headed toward eternity—plowed and replowed in the same field. Truly another civilization beyond man, nature herself, a vast lawless mindprint shattering traditional conceptions.

Thoreau, in his final journals, had said that the ancients with their gorgons and sphinxes could imagine more than existed. Modern men, by contrast, could not imagine so much as exists. For more than one hundred years that statement has stood to taunt us. Every succeeding year has proved Thoreau right. The one great hieroglyph, nature, is as unreadable as it ever was and so is her equally wild and unpredictable offspring, man. Like Thoreau, the examiner of lost and fragile surfaces of flint, we are only by indirection students of man. We are, in actuality, students of that greater order known as nature. It is into nature that man vanishes. "Wildness is a civilization other than our own," Thoreau had ventured. Out of it man's trail had wandered. He had come with the great ice, drifting before its violence, scavenging the flints it had dropped. Whatever he was now, the ice had made him, the breath from the dank door, great cold, and implacable winters.

Thoreau in the final pages of *Walden* creates a myth about a despised worm who surmounts death and bursts from his hidden chamber in a wooden table. Was the writer dreaming of man, man freed at last from the manacles of the ice? No word of his intention remains, save of his diligent experiments with frozen caterpillars in his study—a man preoccupied with the persistent flame of life trapped in the murderous cold. Is not the real business of the artist to seek for man's salvation, and by understanding his ingredients to make him less of an outlaw to himself, civilize him, in fact, back into that titanic otherness, that star's substance from which he had arisen? Perhaps encamped sufficiently in the great living web we might emerge again, not into the blind snow-covered eye of Walden's winter, but into the eternal spring man dreams of everywhere and nowhere finds.

Man, himself, is Walden's eye of ice and eye of summer. What now makes man an outlaw, with the fox urgent at his heels, is the fact that one of his eyes is gray and wintry and blind, while with the other is glimpsed another world just tantalizingly visible and dismissed as an illusion. What we know with certainty is that a creature with such disparate vision cannot long survive. It was that knowledge which led Thoreau to strain his eyesight till it ached and to record all he saw. A flower might open a man's mind,

TECHNICAL COLLEGE OF THE LOWCOUNTRY
LEARNING RESOURCES CENTER
P. O. BOX 1288 *026811*
100 S. RIBAUT ROAD
BEAUFORT, S. C. 29901

a box tortoise endow him with mercy, a mist enable him to see his own shifting and uncertain configuration. But the alchemist's touchstone in Thoreau was to give him sight, not power. Only man's own mind, the artist's mind, can change the winter in man.

II

There are persons who, because of youthful associations, prefer harsh-etched things for their eyes at morning. The foot of an iron bedstead perhaps, or a weathered beam on the ceiling, an abandoned mine tipple, or even a tombstone. On July 14 of the year 1973, I awoke at dawn and saw above my head the chisel marks on an eighteenth-century beam in the Concord Inn. As I strolled up the street toward the cemetery I saw a few drifters, black and white, stirring from their illegal night's sleep among the gravestones. Later I came to the Thoreau family plot and saw the little yellow stone marked "Henry" that no one is any longer sure indicates the precise place where he lies. Perhaps there is justice in this obscurity because the critics are also unsure of the contradictions and intentions of his journal, even of the classic *Walden*. A ghost then, of shifting features, peers out from between the gravestones, unreal, perhaps uninterpreted still.

I turned away from the early morning damp for a glimpse of the famous pond which in the country of my youth would have been called a lake. I walked its whole blue circumference with an erudite citizen of Concord. It was still an unearthly reflection of the sky, even if here and there beer bottles were bobbing in the shallows. I walked along the tracks of the old railroad where Thoreau used to listen to the telegraph wires. He had an eye for the sharp-edged artifact, I thought. The bobbing bottles, the keys to beer cans, he would have transmitted into cosmic symbols just as he had sensed all past time in the odors of a swamp. "All the ages are represented still," he had said, with nostrils flaring above the vegetation-choked water, "and you can smell them out."

It was the same, he found, with the ashes of Indian campfires, with old bricks and cellarholes. As for arrowheads, he says in a memorable passage, "I landed on two spots this afternoon and picked up a dozen. You would say it had rained arrowheads for they lie all over the surface of America. They lie in the meeting house cellar, and they lie in the distant cowpasture. They are sown like grain. . . . over the earth. Each one," Thoreau writes, "yields me a thought. . . . It is humanity inscribed on the face of the earth. It is a footprint—rather a mindprint—left everywhere. . . .

They are not fossil bones, but, as it were, fossil thoughts forever reminding me of the mind that shaped them. I am on the trail of mind."

Some time ago in a graduate seminar met in honor of the visit of an eminent prehistorian I watched the scholar and his listeners try to grapple with the significance of an anciently shaped stone. Not one of those present, involved as they were with semantic involutions, could render up so simple an expression as "mindprint." The lonely follower of the plow at Concord had provided both art and anthropology with an expression of horizon-reaching application which it has inexplicably chosen to ignore.

Mindprints are what the first men left, mindprints will be what the last man leaves, even if it is only a beer can dropped rolling from the last living hand, or a sagging picture in a ruined house. Cans, too, have their edges, a certain harshness; they too represent a structure of the mind, perhaps even an attitude. Thoreau might have seen that, too. Indeed he had written long ago: "If the outside of a man is so variegated and extensive, what must the inside be? You are high up the Platte river," he admonished, "traversing deserts, plains covered with soda, with no deeper hollow than a prairie dog hole tenanted by owls."

Perhaps in those lines he had seen the most of man's journey through the centuries. At all events he had coined two incomparable phrases, the "mindprint" which marked man's strange passage through the millennia and which differentiated him completely from the bones of all those creatures that lay strewn in the basement rocks of the planet, and that magnificent expression "another civilization," coined to apply to nature. That "civilization" contained for Thoreau the mysterious hieroglyphs left by a deer mouse, or the preternatural winter concealment of a moth's cocoon in which leaves were made to cooperate. He saw in the dancing of a fox on snow-whipped Walden ice "the fluctuations of some mind."

Thoreau had extended his thought-prints to something beyond what we of this age would call the natural. He would read them into nature itself, see, in other words, some kind of trail through that prairie for outlaws that had always intimidated him. On mountain tops, he had realized a star's substance, sensed a nature "not bound to be kind to man." Nevertheless he confided firmly to his diary, "the earth which I have *seen* cannot bury me." He searches desperately, all senses alert, for a way to read these greater hieroglyphs in which the tiny interpretable minds of our forerunners are embedded. We, with a sharper knowledge of human limitations and a devotion to the empirical fact, may deny to ourselves the reality of this other civilization within whose laws and probabilities we exist. Thoreau reposed faith in the consistency of nature's habits, but only up to a point, for he was a student of change.

As Alfred North Whitehead was to remark long afterward, "We are in the world and the world is in us"—a phrase that all artists should contemplate. Something, some law of a greater civilization, sustains nature from moment to moment within and above the void of nonbeing. "I hold," maintains the process philosopher, "that these unities of existence, these occasions of experience are the really real things which in their collective unity compose the evolving universe." In spite of today's emphasis upon the erratic nature of the submicroscopic particle there is, warns Whitehead the mathematician, "no valid inference from mere possibility to matter of fact; or, in other words, from mere mathematics to concrete nature. . . . Apart from metaphysical presupposition there can be no civilization." I doubt if Whitehead had ever perused Thoreau's journals, yet both return to the word "civilization," that strange on–going otherness of interlinked connections that makes up the nature that we know, just as human society and its artistic productions represent it in miniature, even to its eternal novelty.

Now Thoreau was a stay-at-home who traveled much in his mind, both in travel literature and beside Walden Pond. I, by circumstance, directly after delivering a lecture at Concord and gazing in my turn at Walden, was forced immediately to turn and fly west to the badlands and dinosaur–haunted gulches of Montana, some of its natives wild, half–civilized, still, in the way that Thoreau had viewed one of his Indian guides in Maine: "He shall spend a sunny day, and in this century be my contemporary. Why read history, then, if the ages and the generations are now? He lives three thousand years deep into time, an age not yet described by poets." As I followed our mixed-breed Cheyenne, as ambivalent toward us as the savage blood in his veins demanded, it came to me, as it must have come to many others, that seeing is not the same thing as understanding.

One man sees with indifference a leaf fall; another with the vision of Thoreau invokes the whole of that nostalgic world which we call autumn. One man sees a red fox running through a shaft of sunlight and lifts a rifle; another lays a restraining hand upon his companion's arm and says, "Please. There goes the last wild gaiety in the world. Let it live, let it run." This is the role of the alchemist, the true, if sometimes inarticulate artist. He transmutes the cricket's song in an autumn night to an aching void in the heart; snowflakes become the flying years. And when, as archaeologist, he lifts from the encrusting earth those forgotten objects Thoreau called "fossil thoughts," he is giving depth and tragedy and catharsis to the one great drama that concerns us most, the supreme mystery, man. Only man is capable of comprehending all he was and all that he has failed to be.

On those sun-beaten uplands over which we wandered, every chip of quartzite, every patinized flint, gleamed in our eyes as large as the monuments of other lands. Our vision in that thin air was incredibly enhanced and prolonged. Thoreau had conceived of nature as a single reflecting eye, the Walden eye of which he strove to be a solitary part, to apprehend with all his being. It was chance that had brought me in the span of a day to the dinosaur beds of Montana. Thoreau would have liked that. He had always regarded such places as endowed with the vapors of Nox, places where rules were annulled. He had called arrowheads mindprints. What then would he have termed a tooth of *Tyrannosaurus rex* held in my palm? The sign of another civilization, another order of mind? Or that tiny Cretaceous mammal which was a step on the way to ourselves? Surely it represented mind in embryo, our mind, but not of our devising. What would he have called it—that miracle of a bygone moment, the annulment of what had been, to be replaced by an eye, the artist's eye, that nature had never heretofore produced among her creatures? Would these have answered for him on this giant upland, itself sleeping like some tired dinosaur with outspread claws? Would he have simply called it "nature," as we sometimes do, scarcely knowing how to interpret the looming inchoate power out of which we have been born? Or would he have labeled nature itself a mindprint beyond our power to read or to interpret?

A man might sketch Triceratops, but the alphabet from which it was assembled had long since disappeared. As for man, how had his own alphabet been constructed? The nature in which he momentarily resided was a journal in which the script was always changing, like the dancing footprints of the fox on icy Walden Pond. Here, exposed about me, was the great journal Thoreau had striven to read, the business, in the end, that had taken him beyond Walden. He would have been too wise, too close to earth, too intimidated, to have called such a journal human. It was palpably inscribed from a star's substance. Tiny and brief in that journal were the hieroglyphs of man. Like Thoreau, we had come to the world's end, but not to the end of nature, not to the end of time. All that could be read was that we had a past; that was something no other life on the planet had learned. There was, he had also ascertained, a future.

In the meantime, Thoreau would have protested, there is the eye, the sun and the eye. "Nothing must be postponed; find eternity in each moment." But how few of us are endowed to sustain Thoreau's almost diabolical vision. Here and here alone the true alchemist of Jung's thought must come to exist in each of us. It is ours to transmute, not iron, not copper, not gold, but our tracks through nature, see them finally attended by self-knowledge, by the vision of the universal eye, that faculty possessed by the alchemist at Walden Pond.

"Miasma and infection come from within," he once wrote. It was as if he sought the cleanliness of flint patinized by the sun of ages, the artifact, the mindprint from which the mind itself had departed. It is something that perhaps only a few artists like Piranesi have understood amidst cromlechs, shards, and broken cities. It is man's final act as an alchemist to find the philosopher's stone in a desert-varnished flint and to watch himself, his mind, his species, evaporate into the air and sun that once had nourished the dinosaurs. Man alone knows the way he came; man alone is the alchemical animal who can vaporize himself in an utter cleansing, either by the powers of art alone, or, more terribly, by that dread device which began its active life at Los Alamos more than thirty years ago.

On a great hill in Montana on the day I had flown from Walden, I picked up a quartz knife that had the look of ten thousand years about it. It was as clean as the sun and I knew suddenly what Thoreau had been thinking about his arrowheads, his mindprints. They were free at last. They had aged out of human history, out of corruption. They were joined to that other civilization, evidence of some power that ran all through nature. They were a sign now beyond man, like all those other traceries of the frost that Thoreau had studied so avidly for evidence of some greater intelligence.

For just a moment I was back at Walden with a mind beyond infection by man, the mind of an alchemist who knew instinctively how laws might be annulled and great civilizations rise evanescent as toadstools on an autumn night. I too had taken on a desert varnish. I might have been a man but, if so, a man from whom centuries had been flayed away. I was being transmuted, worn down. There was flint by my hand that had not moved for millennia. It had ceased to radiate a message and whatever message I, as man, had carried there from Walden was also forgotten.

I lay among logs of petrified wood and found myself already stiffening. Nature was bound somewhere; the great mind was readying some new experiment but not, perhaps, for man. I sighed a little with the cleanliness of that release. I slept deep under the great sky. I slept sound. For a moment as I drowsed I thought of the little stone marked "Henry" in the Concord cemetery. He would have known, I thought—the great alchemist had always known—and then I slept. It was Henry who had once written "the best philosophy is all untrue," untrue, that is, for man. Across an untamed prairie one's footprints must always be altering, that was the condition of the world, the only one that mattered, the only one for art.

III

But why, some midnight questioner persisted in my brain, why had he left that sunny doorway of his hut in Walden for unknown mysterious business? Had he not written as though he had settled down forever? Why had Channing chronicled Thoreau's grievous disappointments? What had he been seeking and how had it affected him? If Walden was the opening chapter of a life, might not there still be a lurking message, a termination, a final chapter beyond his recorded death?

It was evident that he had seen the whole of American culture as copper-tinted by its antecedents, its people shadowy and gigantic as figures looming indistinctly in some Indian-summer haze. He had written of an old tree near Concord penetrated by a flying arrow with the shaft still attached. Some of the driving force of that flint projectile still persisted in his mind. Perhaps indeed those points that had once sung their message through every glade of the eastern woodland had spoken louder than the telegraph harp to which his ears had been attuned at Walden. Protest as he would, cultivate sauntering as he would, abhor as he would the rootless travelers whose works he read by lamplight, he was himself the eternal traveler. On the mountains of New Hampshire he had found "small and almost uninhabited ponds, apparently without fish, sources of rivers, still and cold, strange as condensed clouds." He had wandered without realizing it back into the time of the first continental ice recession.

"It is not worth the while to go around the world to count the cats in Zanzibar," he once castigated some luckless explorer, but why then this peering into lifeless tarns or engrossing himself with the meteoritic detritus of the Appalachians? Did he secretly wish to come to a place of no more life, where a man might stiffen into immobility as I had found myself freezing into the agate limbs of petrified trees in Montana? A divided man, one might say with surety. The bold man of abrasive village argument, the defender of John Brown, the advocate of civil disobedience, the spokesman who supplied many of the phrases which youthful revolutionaries hurled at their elders in the sixties of this century, felt the world too large for him.

As a college graduate he wept at the thought of leaving Concord. Emerson's well-meant efforts to launch him into the intellectual life of New York had failed completely. He admitted that he would gladly fall "into some crevice along with leaves and acorns." To Emerson's dismay he captained huckleberry parties among children and was content to be a rural surveyor, wandering over the farms and woodlots he could not own, save for his all-embracing eye. "There is no more fatal blunderer," he protested, "than he who consumes the greater part of life getting a living." He had emphasized that contemplative view at Walden, lived it, in fact, to the point where the world came finally to accept him as a kind of rural Robinson Crusoe who, as the cities grew, it might prove wise to emulate.

"I sat in my sunny doorway," he ruminated, "from sunrise till noon, rapt in a revery, amidst the pines and hickories and sumachs, in undisturbed solitude and stillness, while the birds sang around or flitted noiseless through the house, until by the sun falling in at my west window, or the noise of some traveller's wagon on the distant highway, I was reminded of the lapse of time. I grew in those seasons like corn in the night."

This passage would seem to stand for the serene and timeless life of an Oriental sage, a well-adjusted man, as the psychiatrists of our day would have it. Nevertheless this benign façade is deceptive. There is no doubt that Thoreau honestly meant what he said at the time he said it, but the man was storm-driven. He would not be content with the first chapter of his life; he would, like a true artist, dredge up dreams even from the bottom of a pond.

In the year 1837 Thoreau confided abruptly to his journal: "Truth strikes us from behind, and in the dark." Thoreau's life was to be comparatively short and ill-starred. Our final question must, therefore, revolve, not about wanderings in autumn fields, not the drowsing in pleasant doorways where time stood still forever, but rather upon the leap of that lost arrow left quivering in an ancient oak. It was, in symbol, the hurtling purposeful arrow of a seemingly aimless life. It has been overlooked by Thoreau's biographers, largely because they have been men of the study or men of the forest. They have not been men of the seashore, or men gifted with the artist's eye. They have not trudged the naturalist's long miles through sea sand, where the war between two elements leaves even the smallest object magnified, as the bleached bone or broken utensil can be similarly magnified only on the dead lake beaches of the west.

Thoreau had been drawn to Cape Cod in 1849, a visit he had twice repeated. It was not the tourist resort it is today. It was still the country of men on impoverished farms, who went to sea or combed the beaches like wreckers seeking cargo. On those beaches, commented Thoreau, in a posthumous work which he was never destined to see in print, "a house was rarely visible . . . and the solitude was that of the ocean and the desert combined." The ceaseless roar of the surf, the strands of devil's-apron, the sun jellies, the stories of the drowned cast on the winter coast awoke in Thoreau what must have been memories of Emerson's shipwrecked friend Margaret Fuller. Here, recorded the chronicler, was a wilder, less human nature. Objects on the beach, he noted, were always more grotesque and dilated than upon approach they proved to be. A cast-up pair of gloves suggested the reality of hands.

Thoreau's account in *Cape Code* of the Charity House to which his wanderings led him takes on a special meaning. I think it embodies something of a final answer to Channing's question about Thoreau's disappointment in his fellow men. Published two years after his death, it contains his formulation of the end of his business, or perhaps I should say of his quest. Hidden in what has been dismissed as a mere book of travel is an episode as potentially fabulous as Melville's great white whale.

First, however, I must tell the story of another coast because it will serve to illuminate Thoreau's final perception. A man, a shore dweller on Long Island Sound, told me of his discovery in a winter dawn. All night there had been a heavy surf and freezing wind. When he came to stroll along his beach at morning he had immediately seen a lifeboat cast upon the shingle and a still, black figure with the eastern sun behind it on the horizon. Gripped by a premonition he ran forward. The seaman in oilskins was alone and stiffly upright. A compass was clutched in his numb fingers. The man was sheeted in ice. Ice over his beard, his clothing, his hands, ice over his fixed, open eyes. Had he made the shore alive but too frozen to move? No one would ever know, just as no one would ever know his name or the sinking vessel from which he came. With desperate courage he had steered a true course through a wild night of breakers only to freeze within sight of help.

In those fishing days on Cape Cod, Thoreau came to know many such stories—vessels without weather warnings smashed in the winter seas, while a pittance of soaked men, perhaps, gained the shore. The sea, the intolerable sea, tumbled with total indifference the bodies of the dead or the living who were tossed up through the grinding surf of winter. These were common events in the days of sail.

The people who gained a scant living along that coast entertained, early in the nineteenth century, the thought that a few well-stocked sheds, or "Charity Houses," might enable lost seamen who made the shore to warm and feed themselves among the dunes till rescued. The idea was to provide straw and matches and provender, supervised and checked at intervals by some responsible person. Impressed at first by this signal beneficence of landsmen, Thoreau noted the instructions set down for the benefit of mariners. Finally, he approached one such Charity House. It appeared, he commented, "but a stage to the grave." The chimney had fallen. As he and his companion wished to gain an idea of a "humane house," they put their eyes, by turns, to a knothole in the door. "We had," Thoreau comments ironically, "some practice at looking inward—the pupil becomes enlarged. Nature is never so dark that a patient eye may not prevail over it."

So there, at last, he saw the end of his journey, of the business begun at Walden. He was peering into the Charity House of man, upon a Cape Cod beach. For frozen, shipwrecked mariners he saw a fireplace with no matches, no provisions, no straw upon the floor. "We looked," he said, "into the bowels of mercy, and for bread we found a stone." Shivering like castaways, "we looked through the knothole into that night without a star, until we concluded it was not a *humane* house at all." The arrow Thoreau had followed away from Walden had pierced as deep as Captain Ahab's lance. No wonder the demoniacal foxes leaping at Thoreau's window had urged him to begone. He had always looked for a crevice into the future. He had peered inward instead. It was ourselves who were rudimental men.

Recently I had a letter from one of my students who is working in the Arctic and who has a cat acquired somewhere in his travels. The cat, he explained to me, hunts in the barrens behind the Eskimo village. Occasionally it proudly brings in a lemming or a bird to his hut. The Eskimo were curious about the unfamiliar creature.

"Why does he do that?" my friend was asked.

"Because he is a good cat," my student explained. "He shares his game."

"So, so." The old men nodded wisely. "It is true for the man and for the beast—the good man and the good beast. They share, yes indeed. They share the game."

I think my young quick-witted friend had momentarily opened the eye of winter. Before laying aside his letter, I thought of the eye of Walden as I had seen it under the summer sun. It was the sharing that had impressed the people of the ice and it was a great sharing of things seen that Thoreau had attempted at his pond. A hundred years after his death people were still trying to understand what he was about. They were still trying to get both eyes open. They were still trying to understand that the town surveyor had brought something to share with his fellows, something that, if they partook of it, might transpose them to another world.

I had thought, staring across an angular gravestone at Concord and again as I held my wind-varnished flint in Montana, that "sharing" could be the word. It was appropriate, even though Thoreau in a final bitterness had felt sharing to be as impoverished as the Charity House for sailors—a knothole glimpse into the human condition. How then should the artist see? By an eye applied to a knothole? By a magnification of sand-filled gloves washed up on a beach? Could this be the solitary business that led Thoreau on his deathbed to mutter, whether in irony or confusion, "one world at a time"?

This is the terror of our age. How should we see? In what world are we? For we have fallen out of nature and see sometimes more and sometimes less. We see the past, the looming future, and then, so fearfully is the eye confused, that it stares inverted into a Charity House that appears to reflect a less than human heart. Is this Thoreau's final surrealist vision, his glance through the knothole into the "humane house"? It would appear at least to be a glimpse from one of those two great alternating eyes at Walden Pond from which in the end he had fled—the blind eye of winter and that innocent blue pupil beside which he had once drowsed when time seemed endless. Both are equally real, as the great poets and prophets have always known, but it was Thoreau's tragic destiny to see with eyes strained beyond endurance man subsiding into two wrinkled gloves grasping at the edge of infinity. It is his final contribution to literature, the final hidden conclusion of an unwritten life whose first chapter Morris had rightly diagnosed as Walden.

There is an old biblical saying that our days are prolonged and every vision fails us. This I would dispute. The vision of the great artist does not fail. It sharpens and refines with age until everything extraneous is pared away. "Simplify," Thoreau had advocated. Two gloves, devoid of flesh, clutching the stones of the ebbing tide become, transmuted, the most dreadful object in the world.

"There has been nothing but the sun and eye from the beginning," Thoreau had written when his only business was looking and he grew, as he expressed it, "like corn in the night." The sun and the eye are the two aspects of nature which are irremediably linked. But the eye of man constitutes an awesome crystal whose diffractions are far greater than those of any Newtonian prism.

We see, as artists, as scientists, each in his own way, through the inexorable lens we cannot alter. In a nature which Thoreau recognized as unfixed and lawless anything might happen. The artist's endeavor is to make it happen—the unlawful, the oncoming world, whether endurable or mad, but shaped, shaped always by the harsh angles of truth, the truth as glimpsed through the terrible crystal of genius. This is the one sure rule of that other civilization which we have come to know is greater than our own. Thoreau called it, from the first, "unfinished business," when he turned and walked away from his hut at Walden Pond.

Part of a Winter

George Sibley

I should not talk so much about myself if there were anybody else whom I knew as well. Unfortunately, I am confined to this theme by the narrowness of my experience. Moreover, I, on my side, require of every writer, first or last, a simple and sincere account of his own life, and not merely what he has heard of other men's lives; some such account as he would send to his kindred from a distant land; for if he has lived sincerely it must have been in a distant land to me.

THOREAU, *Walden*

In the fall of 1971, I made a short move, from just inside the outermost boundary of the modern civilized world to a point just beyond that boundary: together with my wife and yearling son, I moved from Crested Butte to a cabin at the foot of Gothic Mountain, eight miles north of Crested Butte, in what amounts to a large clearing in the Gunnison National Forest.

I lived there with Barbara and Sam for most of four years—four winters in all, though we were away one summer. In the summer of 1974 we were joined by a daughter, Sarah—born right there, in the woods, at home, in the cabin. During those years we were connected with the rest of the human world by a moderately decent dirt road . . . or connected until the snows came. Then, for the duration of the winter, we were a small island of human life in an otherwise nonhuman world, six miles by ski from the nearest phone, grocery store, bar or negotiable road.

Our life there, from the start, was a "retreat." We never thought of it as an "alternative." We knew that our "real" world was the one we call civilized, even though our retreat was specifically from many manifestations of that world. We knew that we would eventually be back in that world,

From *Mountain Gazette* no. 41 (January 1976). © 1976 by George Sibley.

even though one year in the woods seemed to lead to another and another and another. . . .

We went to the woods without knowing exactly why we were doing it. We were there in a more or less "official" capacity as winter caretakers for a summer biological field station located in what was once the mining town of Gothic. But ours was a position that had not existed to be filled until we conspired with the directors of the field station to create it, so we could hardly say we were there for the job.

We told friends who asked that we were living in the woods because it was the only place we could work—Barbara carving and me writing— that was both cheap and quiet. And we *were* there to work. We had decided to leave Crested Butte, in part, because we both felt cast in forms that no longer demanded much from us. I was editing a newspaper that seemed increasingly limited by the pedestrian news available, and Barbara was carving wooden signs on flat boards. We both wanted to add another dimension or two to our work. The cabin in the woods seemed ideal; and to some extent, it was.

We had money enough at that time to lay in nine months of groceries, we had a rent-free sixteen-by-twenty-foot cabin, we had no jobs to go to, and we were six miles from our car and all other forms of urban inconvenience. There was nothing for *me* to do up there except, as I once heard a writer say, "sit down at the typewriter every morning and either write or do penance."

And, of course, there were the chores: wood to gather and cut, coal to haul from the coal pile and the daily water to carry from the spring— five or ten gallons a day, or about two flushes of the modern toilet. Doing the chores, we got to know the woods a little.

I did all the chores on snowshoes. (To do the work on skis would have been a little like trying to plow a field using a Ford Mustang for a tractor.) Usually, though, within a few days after a storm, the trails to the outhouse, the coal pile and the spring were packed enough to walk on without the snowshoes. In a sense, there in the winter woods, we seemed to be living on an "off-shore island" to the main continent of our human world. Around the cabin where I cut the wood and Sam played and Barbara carved on a nice day, and on narrow "peninsulas" radiating outward from the cabin a ways, we were able to move around in a normal fashion, supported on a snowcrust four or five feet above the ground. But always surrounding that small human island was an ocean. . . .

I have watched a snowdrift build up outside the outhouse during a three-day wind, and I now know what it must be like to watch the formation of a wave in slow motion. I've fallen down in six to eight feet of unpacked snow and known for a split-second what a drowning man must feel. And I've seen what the slow, viscid flow of snow does to young trees, even on a gradual slope . . . an ocean indeed.

The wilderness skier who does not think of his skis the way a sailor thinks of his boat is probably courting a rude awakening. I know a man who once went out on a snowmobile without taking the sailor's precautions . . . his machine broke down less than a half-mile out, but it took him over an hour to negotiate the distance back; he was over his head in snow and found that the only way he could make his way back was to lie down, and in a modified rolling fashion, *swim*.

This sense of living on an island in an ocean required more than a physical adjustment. On the mainland, one is not especially aware of the action along the shoreline, the building up and the tearing down; but on a small island one learns quickly that a "conscious rationale" is a sand castle to be built only above the tideline.

When we set out deliberately to "visit the woods," we tend to go out to "appreciate them for what they are" in much the same, consciously directed way that we go out to log them for the timber they are.

And if, during our visits to the woods, we find the woods impressing themselves on us in some way we don't particularly appreciate—a branchful of snow down the neck of an "ill-designed" jacket, a sudden small storm that gets us uncomfortably wet, a soggy frost that soaks our bag—we go back to civilization and buy or invent something to make us more waterproof, snowproof, accidentproof and, finally, natureproof, so that on our next trip into the woods we will be better able to appreciate nature the way we want to appreciate it.

Because we find our civilized lives chaotic, we look for order outside the forms and structures of civilization—in the woods, on the ocean, in what we call, in a self-exclusive way, "the natural world." And we plan for order. There are, of course, certain things we can't plan for, so the success of our wilderness experience depends on several things not happening: accidents, unforeseeable unpleasant events (such as a three-day drizzle) and—maybe this should top the list—encounters with other people wanting to appreciate alone the same things we want to appreciate alone. If we succeed in planning for every foreseeable eventuality, and if nothing unforeseen happens—if, in other words, everything is unnaturally pleasant—then we can come back refreshed, renewed and ready to return to our disorderly, unkempt, tangled, seat-of-the-pants-and-scrap-for-a-place civilization . . . where we will spend every evening all week planning, plotting, finding the maps, marking the routes, cleaning and preparing the equipment, waterproofing the boots and getting ready for another visit to "the natural world" where there is *real order.* . . .

But actually living in the woods for an extended period of time—more than half a year—even those first sustained, superconscious, month-long highs give way to the old off-and-on, sloppy, low-consciousness habits of "civilized life."

Whether your daily routine of survival means going to the job that brings in the money that pays the furnace bills or hauling down and cutting up the dead aspen trees that fulfill the same function, a routine eventually is a routine. And the longer we perform a routine, the less we do it "like a warrior," as Don Juan would say, and the more we tend to sort of sleepwalk through it. Daydreaming our way through the urban world, we are setting ourselves up to get hit by a wayward car; out in the woods we might fall into a hole in the snow and come up in the ocean.

Along with the physical liabilities associated with daydreaming and sleepwalking also comes a certain psychic vulnerability: too much passive participation in routine quite literally erodes our consciousness, our ability to act creatively in the context of our environment. Our life becomes a dream in which good and bad and indifferent things happen to us, but in which we don't "happen" to anything at all.

So while I went to the woods confident that I "knew my way around" and "appreciated the woods for what they were," it wasn't until I became less conscious of my surroundings that my surroundings began to impress themselves on me in subtle ways. . . . There was that first winter's wood-getting, for example.

We had a coal-and-wood heating stove for our cabin—Dirty Gertie, the old potbelly I had used in the Crested Butte *Chronicle* office. Our plan had been to stock coal for the winter, but for a number of reasons, a coal strike among them, the coal delivery had not been made on that day when the sky delivered the first big snow, closing the road for the winter. And that left me with no option but to strap on the snowshoes every day or so and head up into the woods with a bowsaw to bring down a couple of dead standing trees.

Two thirty-foot dead aspens are not much for weight, but trying to maneuver dead trees and snowshoes through a dense stand of live trees in five feet of loose snow teaches a lot about subfreezing sweating, loud swearing and the kind of childish behavior that might bring one to break a knuckle against an aspen that won't even flatter you by quaking. Those daily slogging trips became my real introduction to the woods.

As the first winter wore on, my search for the daily dead aspen took me further and further from the cabin. My trails branched out like the map of a tree among trees. Since it was easier to try to drag today's trees down as much of the trail left by yesterday's trees as possible, I moved out like a railroad, with trunk lines, secondaries and, finally, spurs and sidings to every dead standing tree with a diameter larger than three inches. January was cold as hell that winter, but almost snowless, and following one of my "spurs" off to a new "siding" one day, I was surprised to come upon a fresh stump and a dead-end trail . . . It took me a moment to realize it was just me arriving again where I had already been.

In the course of covering that mountain slope that winter, with that kind of thoroughness, I began to observe on the conscious level what a forester could have told me in a few minutes about the life and death of a forest. Where I had initially been aware only of a broad expanse of aspen trees—some alive and beautiful, some dead and useful—I found myself seeing from more than one approach the huge old burnt stumps of a former forest, and the new spruce and pine beginning to spread clumpwise: I could see that, in a frame of reference hardly relevant to my own, this aspen wood was a transitional forest between two evergreen forests; and while the aspen grew, spread, and died quickly in a time of their own, from an objective (un-aspen) perspective, they were merely an emergency measure in the big picture, like sandbags on the eroding levee. The aspens laced the slope together with their shallow, laterally-spreading roots; they gave shelter, shade and eventually a rich layer of leafmold to the forest floor where the new conifers were taking sturdy root in a time frame of *their* own . . . it all worked so well, it might have been planned, a rational regime by a rational god.

But something else happened that winter which, while not necessarily negating that conscious apprehension of "rationality" in the forest, certainly added another perspective to my "appreciation" of the woods. It was a small thing—maybe too small to even talk about. But what the hell. . . .

According to those who study the phenomenology of sleep and dreaming, there is a certain kind of peculiar nightmare produced by the deeper levels of sleep—one accompanied by almost none of the REM (Rapid-Eye-Movement) that accompanies most dreaming. The "nightmare" tends to be a recurring dream, jolting enough to awaken the dreamer. But once awake, in recalling these dreams in conscious words and images, people see them as innocuous and static pictures—an empty hallway with closed doors, a wall lined with shelves of books . . . no motion, no perceivable presence, but an image somehow overhung with a palpable imminence so strong that it causes our protective consciousness to jerk us out of our sleep, to keep us from going *too* far. For our own good, presumably.

One day late that winter, I was kind of sleepwalking my way through the woods thinking about something else, when I was suddenly jerked into awareness of my immediacy, much as I have been suddenly pulled out of sleep by my own reaction to a dream. I found myself in a grove of conifers, a place in the woods where I had never wandered before. I will not say that I was frightened; I was just . . . disoriented for a moment. I gathered my wits (think of a shepherd rounding up his sheep), and discovered that everything was fine, nothing out of the ordinary: it was a sunny, quiet and mellow afternoon; there wasn't so much as a hare turning; the sky was blue and it wasn't snowing; and I was in a beautiful spot, all things considered. Yet I had just experienced the daydreamer's equivalent of that deep-sleep nightmare.

I tried to figure it out rationally, having nothing better to do that afternoon. The grove itself was small—not more than a hundred yards long by, maybe, thirty or fifty yards across, sitting on a small glacial bench on the hillside. But it was not a grove of the coming forest; it was part of the older forest, the one that had been burned once, then logged out to build Gothic. The oldest trees in the grove were not so large as the huge old burnt stumps that occurred here and there among the aspens, but they were definitely "virgin" in the sense that they preceded the advent of the axe.

One of the more sensible aspects of a forest fire (more sensible than a good, clean clear-cutting operation) is its inefficiency: the fire likes the old and pest-ridden parts of a forest, but often tends to go right over the top of young healthy groves, leaving nothing worse than some needle singe and a few spots of burned bark that make the tree more vulnerable to eventual invasion by the bark beetle. But the grove lives, and such a spot "remembers" the old forest—through its seed—and regenerates what it remembers; this is how forests managed to perpetrate themselves before there were Principles of Forest Management and a Forest Service to administer them.

But there I was, orderly rationalizing, in orderly retreat, from . . . *what?* Was it a sudden fleeting nightmare? Or just the beginning of a nightmare, or perhaps only the memory of the beginning of a nightmare. It was as if a projector with faulty wiring had started up only to immediately throw a protective circuit breaker (just as in those deep dreams when the breaker is thrown to keep us from approaching the one door in that silent hallway, the one book on the shelves in the wall . . . the one we must never open).

For just the blink of an eye I saw it flash before me: *the forest remembers!*

Had I left the woods after that first winter I might have remembered only that: one beautiful afternoon in a beautiful place when it suddenly occurred to me out of that clear blue sky that (as any geneticist could have told me) the forest has a memory and regenerates the new forest out of what is "remembered" from the old one.

But I was to stay in the woods for three more winters. And as I worked in the woods the woods began to work in me. *What* does the forest remember? And deeper into the subconscious, past those protective circuit breakers, what do *I* remember that the forest also remembers?

It was something to ponder during the slow part of a winter.

> At six I passed James Collins and his family on the road. One large bundle held their all—bed, coffee-mill, looking-glass, hens—all but the cat; she took to the woods and became a wild cat, and, as I learned afterwards, trod in a trap set for woodchucks, and so became a dead cat at last.
>
> THOREAU, *Walden*

The Collins's cat. And the Collins family: James Collins, you might remember, was the Irish railroad worker who sold his trackside shanty to Henry Thoreau in 1845, who in turn used the boards to build his more famous shanty at Walden Pond. We could do a kind of "St. Ives" riddle on the scene on the road that morning: As Henry Thoreau was going to the woods / he met a family with their household goods . . . et cetera . . . kids, wives, sacks of goods how many were going to the woods?

America, for sure, was not going to the woods at the time; and James Collins and his family were on their way to America, for better or worse. In the case of James himself, we can probably imagine the move was definitely for the worse; but somewhere in that growing brood of responsibility, he didn't quite associate with his penchant for hard drink and soft women (alluded to by Thoreau as a quality of all Irishmen), there was probably a sober little kid whose bible was the gospel according to Horatio Alger. . . . Now we look at our heritage from James Collins's son Tom, and there is a tendency to want to say it might have been better for us all had they all gone to the woods with Henry that morning.

But getting back to our riddle, it is worth noting that Henry Thoreau wasn't the only one going to the woods that day. In gaining his home he had cost the Collins's cat her home, so we can infer that both he and the cat took to the woods at the same time: Henry to *observe* the wildness there, and the cat to *participate* in it. And in thinking about "life in the woods," it is as important to weigh the subjective experience of the participants as it is their more objective observations. . . . Thoreau's conclusion that "the preservation of life" is to be found in wildness might not register on the cat, who, after all, died because of it. As for me, I would have to say that both my reasons for going to the woods and my experiences there must lie somewhere between Thoreau's and the cat's.

During my time in the woods, when I wasn't working at the typewriter, or working in the woods, or in the woods being worked on, I was usually reading. Unlike Thoreau in the woods, I did not read the classics—at least, not the classics *he* read in the woods. But I did read Thoreau in the woods—or reread him, to be exact.

I talk to myself a lot, and like anyone who has ever taken his education a little seriously, I talk to myself in many voices. Out in the woods, it was only natural that one of those voices would be Henry Thoreau's. I first read *Walden* thirteen years ago in college—jamming through it in one of those terrible English courses that pack a year's worth of reading into four months (which must be shared with two or three other courses doing the same thing). I can't say I got a damn thing out of it that time around, except part of an "A." But I read it "Thoreauly" that first winter out in the woods, and I have been reading from it off and on every winter since. Once you have been all the way through it, *Walden* is a fine book to pick up on the way to the outhouse. . . .

I will say right off that Henry Thoreau and I did not have an easy relationship out in the woods. For one thing, there was a very basic difference between our lives in the woods, a difference that often made the lessons he sermonized out of his experiences seem irrelevant to me. Thoreau lived alone in the woods and I didn't. And the nature of nature being what it is, a bachelor's observations on that "wildness" in which lies "the preservation of life" can't be regarded as covering the whole picture, not so long as it continues to take two, a man and a woman, in some kind of compatible relationship to "preserve life."

If Henry had seemed the least bit aware of this basic fact of life, it would not have bothered me as it does. But to the contrary, Henry not only seemed totally unaware of the fact that the stork didn't bring him, he seemed to go out of his way to imply that only an Irishman could ever be so stupid as to get himself in a family way.

I can't read the chapter on "Baker Farm" without getting really pissed off at Henry—him and his smug sense of superiority toward men with families, like the Irishman John Field. I wish he were alive now, so he might come by George Sibley's cabin, as he did John Field's, and tell me that if my family and I "would live simply, we might all go a-huckleberrying in the summer for our amusement"! Or inform me that if I had "arithmetic enough" I might be able to live as he did:

> In an hour or two, without labor, but as a recreation, I could,
> if I wished, catch as many fish as I should want for two days,
> or earn enough money to support me for a week.

Sure, Henry! And probably Henry harbored some simplistic notion that, if he could earn enough in "an hour or two" to support himself for a week, then I should be able to do as much for a family of four in half a day or a day, and have the rest of the time to live "as deliberately as Nature."

Anyone with a family knows that this simply isn't so. There isn't any one reason why it isn't so; there are a million. And the reasons are as tangled and interwoven as Nature herself, so that dealing with one usually pulls forth a train of a dozen or so more. No sooner do you start out a-huckleberrying than the baby shits in her pants and starts squirming and crying. The delay from diaper-changing makes the four-year-old impatient; he fusses for a moment, then wanders off and deliberately falls in the stream. Whoever is changing the baby yells at the other parent for not having kept an eye on the other kid. And so it goes. If human nature is to be regarded, as it must be, as a manifestation of nature—with a capital "N"—there is no basis at all for assuming that Nature is "deliberate" *all* the time.

Reading *Walden* in the woods—after the snows had come and I was isolated from any opportunity to pursue an honest job in town—I began to feel a real affinity, even a warmth, for those Irishmen whom Thoreau was always putting down—John Field, James Collins and the others whose "shadows had no halo about them." And the warmth I felt for them was one I cannot feel for Thoreau himself.

"Alas!" he says, "the culture of an Irishman is an enterprise to be undertaken with a sort of moral bog hoe." I know exactly what he means, but I can't share his sense of superiority. Being a family man, and therefore no longer my own man, I am more Irish than an observer of the Irish, and I am well enough acquainted with the "moral bog hoe."

It is easy enough to describe and define that "bog hoe" Thoreau speaks of—it is something that you find yourself behind without particularly liking it, but something you stay behind anyway. My own bog hoe has most often been a hammer, driving other men's nails for other men's houses— even more galling, other men's *second* houses in Crested Butte, where I cannot afford my *first* house. After I had the good fortune to find the caretaker position in the woods, time behind the bog hoe was minimized; but I know the tool, and I can only agree when Henry sermonizes on the negative quality of such weaponry. A bog hoe civilization is a lousy civilization.

But what is old Henry Huckleberry's solution? "Simplify, simplify! . . . I say, let your affairs be as two or three, and not a hundred or a thousand; instead of a million count half a dozen, and keep your accounts on your thumbnail." But Henry, in this grand burdensome sprawl of family, friends, mindborn structures, and all the peripheral complications just waiting for the light of attention, what are the criteria for elimination in editing from a million to half a dozen? Bad as it all can look at times, this unheavenly host of confusion is my life—and do I *really* want a life I can fit on my thumbnail, or do I just occasionally think it might be nice?

Eventually, I can only throw up my hands and walk away laughing, to join the Brotherhood of the Bog Hoe down at the bar where we put our illusion of escape from complication in a glass, not on our thumbnails. It is not we who lack "arithmetic enough to carry through" Henry's life; it is he who lacks the geometry to help us in ours.

Yes, I wish it had been my cabin instead of John Field's that Henry graced with his guest lecture, because I would like to have had the chance to tell Henry how fortunate he was in never having met anyone like Barbara, or known anyone like our young son Sam, and watched the entangling complications multiply out of hand. It causes one to suffer the illusion that the nature of Nature is not to simplify at all. The family of man, from the ancient bog of protozoic slime to the modern bog of cultural chaos, tends to form the notion that the whole, unfolding thrust of life has consistently followed the exact opposite dictum: Complexify, complexify, complexify. . . .

I would have called Henry's attention to what Henry James said about the "young unmarried ladies" dominating the English novel in Thoreau's century, noting that "half of life is a sealed book to young unmarried ladies, and how can a novel be worth anything that deals with only half of life?"

I would have confronted Henry (Thoreau) with the obvious comparison to "young unmarried men," and wondered with Henry (James) whether his words could ever be regarded as any more than "a good thing for virgins and boys."

And I could only conclude, at the end of this imagined debate, that my life in the woods was not in the spirit of Thoreau's, but was in a spirit of my own that was often in necessary contention with the shadow of Thoreau.

Someone might argue at this point that I am picking on Thoreau unfairly, that his being so obviously full of shit at Baker Farm doesn't invalidate what he has to say in the woods *outside* of Baker Farm, where even the most bogged-down Irishman occasionally finds himself alone.

But, unfortunately, what we might call the "virgin bachelor attitude" seems to carry over into Henry's reflections on just about everything; and while his observations are not necessarily invalid at all, they are not all that complete, either.

There are his reflections on "Nature," for example. Obviously, a man who is a solitary bachelor is different "by nature" from a man who is not. But when you spell it with a capital letter, as Henry spells "Nature," there is an apparent attitude of generality, a sense of universals, as though the idea of Nature there expressed should be good enough for all.

In looking around at a "Nature" which he obviously wants to hold up as an example to his "unnatural" neighbors, Thoreau has a nice eye for detail, and he doesn't appear to edit the nonhuman aspects of Nature very much. He even dwells at some length on—or near—a dead horse at one point in his rambles. A Sunday-supplement nature poet would leave out the dead horse.

But the bachelor fastidiousness shows up when he addresses himself to human Nature. The Irishman in me has always wondered, for example, why a man so intent on itemizing his expenditures and daily doings down to the half-penny and the half-hour never tells us where his outhouse is, or how much it cost, or how he built it, or if he even had or needed one. Did he sneak out behind trees? Run over to Emerson's?

There are possible clues to this enigma throughout *Walden*. One could make certain assumptions, for example, from such a statement as, "The better part of the man is soon plowed into the soil for compost."

Still, if it turns out that one of the ways in which Thoreau "simplified" was by doing it in a coffee can and dumping it at night down the outhouse of one of those farmer/neighbors whom he treated so condescendingly during the day, then we should know about it.

I am not trying to suggest that Thoreau should have given priority to, uh, covering his natural functions rather than that which he did cover in such detail; but are not these the kind of "essential facts of life" that we all have to "front" eventually?

Certainly had Thoreau gone *today* before the Concord Planning and Zoning Commission with plans for a basic twenty-eight-dollar-twelve-and-a-half-cent structure, he would have had to "front this essential fact of life." Such august boards and commissions have absolutely no official interest in what a man "intends to live for"; but they are almost obsessed with what he intends to do with his shit.

Barbara and I happen to have a remote, ten-acre mining claim, in case we ever decide we *really* want to live in the woods. If I wanted to put in an outhouse there, according to the law I would have to lug enough cement up on my back to build a concrete vault, and I'll leave it to your imagination how I might feel about emptying it when full. An outhouse properly placed on that claim would have approximately five hundred acres of rock and shady soil to leach through before getting close to anything other than one small, intermittent stream.

I have decided that, when and if we ever decide to put up a cabin, or even a tent, on that piece of land, I am going to build an outhouse over a plain dirt hole; but unlike Henry, I am not going to try to hide my humanness under a bushel. And I am prepared to take my case all the way to the Supreme Court, if necessary. The world is going to concede the fact that George Sibley's elemental eliminations are as much an acceptable and assimilable part of Nature as the old grizzly's bar-stool.

It might seem that, if Henry was remiss in deliberately avoiding the whole fabric of human Nature, I am going overboard in deliberately displaying its more basic aspects at the expense of the "whole human life" in its nobler manifestations. But a father of two children under five knows something about the roots of conscious human nobility that no bachelor could be sensitive to: the human animal's first enduring act of consideration to self and society is toilet-training. For our first two years in the woods we were plagued in a kind of a mild but chronic way with feces—from Sam and from the little brown field mice. If we forgot to put the butter or the sugar away in the cupboard, we had to scrape off the mouse turds in the morning; periodically I had to take all the papers out of my desk drawers and empty the droppings, and half the papers had little yellow stains all over them. After two years, Sam accepted personal responsibility for his own shit, while the mice just never learned. The fact that it is human nature to be concerned about our shit elevates us. But that fact that we think it a dirty secret alienates our nature from the rest of Nature. That, you might say, is an unnatural circumstance, as unnatural as the virgin bachelor. Yet who gave us our world? Moses, Saint Paul, and today we would make Henry a saint: will there never be a philosopher we can honor who has also openly washed a diaper in his day?

From "Nature," it is but a short step into another favorite concept of Henry's—"Wildness." That in which (for all except the Collins's cat) Thoreau sees the "preservation of life."

I am sensitive to a differentiation that I am sure Henry would make between his concept of "wildness" and, say, the Congressional definition of "wilderness." Essentially, he would say that "wildness" is found in the "wilderness," but is not at all limited to the wilderness. Henry spent time in the Maine woods, which is wilderness enough for anyone; but he was also quite fond of seeking out and depicting the examples of "wildness" he found in the fields and woodlots right in the midst of the Concord agrarian community. For example:

> I caught a glimpse of a woodchuck stealing across my path, and felt a strange thrill of savage delight, and was strongly tempted to seize and devour him raw; not that I was hungry then, except for that wildness which he represented.

From this and other usage, I would guess that Henry would define the "wild" as anything living or growing in its original natural state, anything not cultivated or domesticated . . . which is a standard, acceptable definition. We can assume that Henry would have felt the same "strange thrill of savage delight," had he seen a chipmunk, a bear or a tiger crossing his path.

But suppose he had seen, instead, a drunk and pissed-off Irishman? I think we can be sure that neither Thoreau nor the Wilderness Society would feel a "strange thrill of savage delight" upon being so confronted. But I can think of no conceivable *reasonable* qualification of the basic definition of "wildness" that would include the woodchuck but exclude the Irishman. Nor can I see anything that would exclude me, nor Henry.

Yet Henry, who never has a bad thing to say about the wild woodchuck, never has a good thing to say about the wild Irishman. And the Irishman, for that matter, wouldn't even have to be drunk and pissed-off— Henry would feel no delight if any person at all, even one sober as a stick, crossed his path in the woods. Rather than wanting to "devour him raw," Henry would pass with some quick comment on the state of evening, then soliloquize about how "men come tamely home at night."

I remember a riddle about the woods from my riddling days. "How far can you go into the woods?" The answer—then—was, "just to the middle—after that, you are coming out of the woods."

That makes sense, as a riddle; but in the actual practical case, I'm not so sure it's true. When you get far enough into the woods, the woods start getting into you; then even if you leave them, you will never come completely out of the woods. . . .

Maybe it is just as well that we moved out of the woods for a while. I was growing concerned about the holes in the bottom of my mind. Or maybe I was growing concerned about the fact that I was growing less concerned about the holes—at any rate, I was starting to get vertigo every time I looked down.

I was able to keep the situation under control, more or less; I could, when I wanted to, tack over the holes with mental business, make up and pin down long lists and little notes, epoxify thoughts and press them around the edges like putty—*but only when I wanted to.* You will know what I mean, if you have ever begun to feel confronted with the early hairline cracks at the foundations of your own mind: at first, the mind panics at the possibility and fights to hide it under a bushel of normalcy. But—according to my theory of non-genetic madness, based on observation—since most conventional adult paranoia is the reaction of a potentially strong mind to a numbingly boring context of reality, the initial panic is gradually replaced by fascination: as the cracks widen, and little bits of the sub-flooring begin breaking away into freefall, there is less of a tendency to take refuge in normalcy, more and more of a temptation to just sit down and watch it all happen, maybe leaning forward a little to look over the end into the growing hole, tempting the vertigo of knowing that, if one just bent over and clasped one's knees, went into what my swimming teacher called the eggroll position, and what others call the fetal position, and toppled, toppled. . . .

But as I said, we've moved down out of the woods, for the time being; moved back to town. I even bought a used lawnmower, as I've always thought there is a positive correlation between the state of man's yard and what he wants his neighbors to think is the state of his mind. You can see by my yard, as I can see by yours: I'm O.K., you're O.K. That guy down the block now, lawn gone to seed, weeds up to the second-story windows, dead cars and dinosaur bones all over his lot, great gray cats and forty-foot blacksnakes slinking in and out of his unpainted garage—something definitely wrong with him; but us . . . these fragments we have shored against our ruins.

Henry, too, returned from the woods after a couple of years—became, as he said, "a sojourner in civilized life again." I have wondered if Henry was beginning to feel troubled by holes in the bottom of his mind, as I was, when he was out in the woods.

I think it is entirely possible that he was. He spent a great deal of his time in the woods making journals and taking notes, which is really only the mind's equivalent of keeping the lawn mowed; and he came up with a pretty tidy picture of "life in the woods" at the end of it all—but still, for one like myself who has been to the middle of the woods only to find that one isn't necessarily coming out by moving on, there is evidence in Henry's writing of subtle erosions. . . .

Living in the woods, working in the woods, going deeper into the woods all the time, if there was an increasing shifting insubstantiality to the ground underfoot, an almost imperceptible downward cant to the terrain, less the aimless chatter of birds and more a kind of humming, funneling silence, the evening's approach and then suddenly the call of an owl . . . well:

> I rejoice that there are owls. Let them do the idiotic and maniacal hootings for men. It is a sound admirably suited to swamps and twilight woods which no day illustrates, suggesting a vast and undeveloped nature which men have not recognized. They represent the stark twilight and unsatisfied thoughts which all have. All day the sun has shone on the surface of some savage swamp, where the single spruce stands hung with usnea lichens, and small hawks circulate above, and the chickadee lisps amid the evergreens, and the partridge and rabbit skulk beneath; but now a more dismal and fitting day dawns, and a different race of creatures awakes to express the meaning to Nature there.

Even if he didn't stay, Henry was there, too. . . .

My bright spots, like the echo, always seem to come when the shadows around me still measure longer than their objects. As the sun climbs in that bland, flawless sky, the morning shine and sparkle seem to burn right off the world, and even the echo loses its quality, although it might continue in a desultory and perfunctory fashion. In the morning, I bellow, "Why?" and a great chorus sings, "Why not!" But at noon, a committee routes down a memo saying, "Why bother . . . ?"

No matter what the season, summer or winter, and no matter where I am, woods or city, it all looks the worst when I can see it best in the strongest light. I always tried to manage what minimal schedule I maintained in the woods so that all the monotonous work fell toward the middle of the day, because the hours from eleven to three aren't worth a damn for anything worth doing. I know why the people in the tropics invented the siesta. I had my writing desk in the darkest corner of the cabin—more by chance than by choice, since that was the only place it fit—but during those hours that belong entirely to the sun, even that corner was no suitable retreat; a kind of opaqueness permeates everywhere except in the thickest and most impenetrable reaches of the oldest forests, and maybe, before it burned down, to the back tables in Frank Starika's bar in Crested Butte.

As for the rest of the woods and the life that sleeps therein, at high noon on a brilliant day I can think of them only in one of three contexts: a postcard, a board-foot estimate, a Wilderness Society proposal. All non-magical, two-dimensional (or merely three), only as great as their paper-work and something of a bore.

I think, during those hours, of a certain mountain near Crested Butte, a mountain with a big southwest-facing cirque with long ridges running along the sides of the bowl. I've been up that mountain, moving through its woods at bare first light and hiking its ridge on a crust in the first flush of dawn to ski that huge cirque, with its precipitous headwall and long, sailing runout. I know it to be as good a mountain as any. But I remember it best as I used to see it from a distance, working as a patrolman at the ski area across the valley. I see, under the scour of the sun, a monstrous shrunken torso, the headwall of the bowl a slumping caved-in chest, the ridges like slack limbs on throne-arms—and there is no head. In the eye of my mind, that mountain looks like a dead god. Or perhaps one of Zelazny's "great slow kings," an ancient wreck that hasn't completed a thought since its head slipped off and crumbled to dust a million solstices ago. Maybe this mountain remembers life, or maybe only dreams of life. But it isn't a life that has to do with me. For the duration of me, *the mountain just sits there*. Skiing down its bowl, I'm not even crab lice to the mountain. I have been halfway to the center of that same mountain in a network of drifts, stopes and shafts that defy description; and its bowels don't even rumble. What do I have to do with the mountain? What does it have to do with me?

Irritated by its unrevealing opaqueness under the strongest light available for conscious study, I might stake a claim and dig holes, rip off its trees like Custer's scalp, climb it and roll down big rocks, mine it for dwarves and dragongold, run lifts up its ridges, sew zippers down every couloir, squeeze it for diamonds or blood, anything to probe it for something to offset the growing evidence of insight that perhaps life exists only to burn off the energy of the galaxy.

I could, if it so possessed me in rage at unrevealing opaqueness, take that shrunk, defunct, eroded godheadless and reduce it to basic rubble, run it down in rivers and spread it in deltas, turn it over to oceans to rub down to sand. Or just do it symbolically, like Cristo: package it up like a pre-Columbian artifact, address it to Timbuktu and leave the rest up to customs and the Postal Service.

The trouble with this is the time it would take: it would cost me my whole allotment, piddling as it is, just getting the project set up. Look at all the man-hours in that *reductio ad absurdum* called the Climax Mine on

Fremont Pass in Colorado—and to get the true picture, you have to include not just the on-site man-hours, but all the in-transit, in-factory, in-board-room, in-showroom, in-kitchen-and-garage man-hours that have been consumed in the voluntary slavery that accepts molybdenum as a "necessity." Even with all that barely conceivable collaboration in our collective American effort to hump that hill off the map, "Climax" is still a ways off. Well, just a ways, perhaps.

But at high noon, on a dull, cloudless, glaring day in the midst of that opaque indifference, I think that I have to do *something* besides just continue to bring in the wood, eat, convert protein and molybdenum, make hay, maintain routines and, generally, do my piss-in-the-ocean passive bit to slowly convert the vital energy of our daily star to the supergravitating mass of a celestial black hole.

Henry doesn't seem to feel that way at all, of course. Henry can sit inside on a rainy afternoon and observe that:

> The gentle rain which waters my beans and keeps me in the house today is not drear and melancholy, but good for me too. Though it prevents my hoeing them, it is of far more worth than my hoeing. If it should continue so long as to cause the seeds to rot in the ground and destroy the potatoes in the low lands, it would still be good for the grass on the uplands, and, being good for the grass, it would be good for me.

This is the kind of thing Thoreau is famous for—and deservedly, for Thoreau wrote some of the finest prose sentences the English language will ever know. Sometimes he says things that sound as though they were chiseled in stone. At other times, he seems to sew living-room-wall "samplers." I can see that last quote hanging on a million walls, in the *Reader's Digest* condensed form, perhaps: "What's good for the grass is good for me . . . Thoreau."

What Thoreau actually seems to be *saying* in that sentiment is that, if the rain ruins the beans, he will be glad to eat the grass. I too would eat grass, but I wouldn't do it gladly; and I would probably vent myself of many ill-considered opinions on the clouds above. I could sooner see Thoreau's sentiment hanging on my wall than hung in my heart—even though it is, in terms of domestic tranquility and fusion with nature, cosmically correct.

Perhaps what's good for the grass *is* good for me, and that is all I need to know about life. But if that is so, then I am sure as hell a freak, a mutant, an evolutionary dead end—and I'm not the only one. If what's good for the grass is good enough for man, why did men ever learn to consciously and deliberately grow beans, and why aren't we still foraging like skunks?

Why indeed. "Consider the lilies of the field, how *they* grow," said another of the great virgin bachelors in the chaotic apogee of another great age; "they neither toil nor spin, yet even Solomon in all his glory was not so arrayed."

"I should be glad," says our virgin bachelor, "if all the meadows on the earth were left in a wild state, if that were the consequence of men's beginning to redeem themselves." Are we only redeemed, then, to the degree that we are passive? Is it the chief end of man to grow in place like the grass, the lilies of the field—to be still and just *be*? Then all the mindborn structures, the sand-castles of conscious rationale, the *Civitas Dei* that is profaned in our groping efforts to realize the complexity of its possibility, these are all nothing but a form of madness, grand delusions that our destiny is something other than merely to "go a-huckleberrying in the summer for our amusement."

Is it the ultimate function of consciousness to prove that consciousness is a mistake? When I look at Crested Butte, Southwestern Colorado, the Rocky Mountains, the world at large, the litter on my desk, I think I must know how Odin, Vili and Ve might have felt, watching the great flow of blood from Ymir fill the abyss.

Now why did we go and do a thing like that? And yet, like Odin, we are compelled to do *something*. *That* is in *our* blood. Judging from present-day sales of *Walden*, Thoreau is responsible for the death of several thousand trees in advocating our redemption through leaving the fields in a "wild state." And how many millions have toiled, spun, built and died in the name of the one who reminded us of the lilies of the field?

We seem to be trapped in an inconceivable paradox. . . .

"Let us," Henry intones, "spend one day as deliberately as Nature . . . settle ourselves, and work and wedge our feet downward through the mud and slush of opinion, and prejudice, and tradition, and delusion, and appearance, that alluvion which covers the globe, till we come to a hard bottom and rocks in place, which we can call *reality,* and say, This is, and no mistake."

I like Thoreau's imagery here—what you might call his "sedimental journey." In essence, he is saying that that which we call civilization is but the detritus of time and trial-by-error, the record of a progression of efforts to deal with problems that are really the alluvial consequence of *prior* efforts to deal with problems that are the alluvial consequence—and so on, back through layer upon layer of symptom-treatments until—bump!—we all at once touch down on the rock-bottom problem that was the seed-irritant for the whole pearled culture.

To put this to a specific, consider the "population problem" (too many people), and consider it as one of those simplified hardline drawings in the geology texts that represent what only the trained eye can easily see in the jumbled wall of the cliff. One reason we have this population problem is because we have been so successful in solving the problems of infant mortality and epidemic disease. These problems in turn were partially the result of the proximity of people following the agricultural revolution that was at least partially an effort to solve the problems endemic to the uncertain and relentless lifestyle of the nomadic hunter/forager peoples. So every time we cover a problem with a solution, the solution becomes a new problem requiring a new solution.

The layers build up until we have to take the sedimental journey to even notice the macro-irony of the fact that all our efforts to solve the problem of a precariously small population have suddenly led to a precariously large population. Here we can draw a heavier line in the text, and so define an age in the geology of civilizations. Here we begin a new age, in which we define the age's problem as being too many people and lay down solution upon solution until someday (we can imagine) we will suddenly discover that again we have a precariously small population. End of another age. It could, of course, be a very short age.

But the problem with Henry's sedimental journey has to do with his assumption that it leads eventually to "a hard bottom with rocks in place, which we can call *reality.*" It is probably important to remember that, while Henry did go to the woods, and did go into the woods as far as the near edge of a "savage swamp," there is nothing to indicate that he actually took the sedimental journey to that hard bottom and brought back samples to prove its existence.

"Let us do this," he says, but in a rhetorical kind of way, not unlike the political Harvard Henries he otherwise disparages. This exhortation, combined with his own lack of details (such a trip surely would be more worth a book than a mere two years on a pond a mile out of Concord), leads me to suspect that he was only putting forth this "hard bottom" as a possibility, hoping that someone else would take fire and go first, so (knowing Henry) he could follow along afterwards and take notes.

Thinking of this—some disciple of Henry's squashing and sludging soundlessly down, down through the alluvium of the civilizations, "through Paris and London, through New York and Boston and Concord, through Church and State, through poetry and philosophy and religion," while Henry monitors the messages coming up—makes me think of that old joke about the kids at the swimming hole having a contest to see who can stay under water the longest . . . "And Jim Collins has been down an hour-and-a-half. . ." And still no bottom, eh, Jim? Well, don't give up. . . .

I would imagine that most of us will agree, and Henry would admit, that no one is ever going to even define or describe such a point *d'appui*, let alone touch down on it. To that extent, his statement is definitely rhetorical. The point itself, or any direct evidence of its existence, is nowhere observable. Therefore, if Henry or anyone else truly believes that there is an external and a priori reality underlying all human and non-human structures, it can *only* be regarded as an article of faith.

What Henry is really asking us to do, then, when he asks us to "spend one day as deliberately as Nature" in order to seek out this "hard bottom with rocks in place," is to accept a convention. And the convention he asks us to accept is practically as old as what we know of our history itself: the conventional belief that beneath all our layers of "sham and appearance," our unrepentant record of prodigality, our debris of sins of ignorance and arrogance, there is a Garden.

But what is most important about the acceptance of such an article of faith is the way in which it is bound to shape and color the believer's entire relationship with the world about him, with "Nature." If a person believes in the existence of this point *d'appui,* this "still point," the hard bottom, then that person's whole perception of the dynamics of life will be grounded thereon.

And if that point, that center, is the Garden, then a number of things are "explained" for an age that seems to have been plagued with bad actions, unforeseen problems and creative forms of destruction: we can "do no right" because we have been evicted from the Garden for playing god. Only if we strip away all our illusions of significant toil, squelch our drive to do, and reaffirm the existence of a well-balanced, ecologically sound and vast eternal plan in which our conscious activity is not only superfluous but quite disruptive, only then can we reenter the Garden with God's blessing and forever after move in peaceful harmony with Nature.

Without the Garden, however, all of this obviously falls apart; it is a pattern which requires a predicating center. But in the wake of developments that were beginning right where Thoreau left off—or, say, right at the edge of the savage swamp from which Thoreau retreated—it is more difficult than ever to cling rationally to the myth of the Garden.

Even as Henry was sounding the depths and taking the measure of Walden Pond (1845–47) with his Garden-centered perceptions, another young man was about halfway through a similar, but larger, venture on the largest ponds, a twenty-year episode of note-taking that would put cracks all through the foundations of Judeo-Christian "Garden-thinking."

That man was Charles Darwin, and just five years after the publication of *Walden,* he brought out the *Origin of the Species.* A serious blow to the nobly tragic view of man as over-reacher fallen from grace, trying to work his way back, this damned theory said there was nothing there particularly worth working our way back to. And, just like a scientist, with cold facts and hard examples, damned Darwin made his theory as hard to disprove as Genesis was *to prove.*

But the world had barely begun to assimilate this information on a conscious level when the physicists started exhibiting their heresies about the nature of matter and energy, talking of building blocks so powerfully small for structures so incredibly large that the image of a father-god work-ing with lumps of clay took on all the characteristics of an illustration for a child's book. The metaphysical strain approached the limits of elasticity during World War I, with the publicity and furor surrounding the publi-cation of Einstein's Theory of General Relativity:

> Nature and Nature's law lay hid in night.
> God said, "Let Newton be" and all was light.
> It did not last: the Devil howling, "Ho!
> Let Einstein be!" restored the status quo.
>
> (Sir John Squire)

And now, even the static metaphorical beauty of the "sedimental jour-ney" is shattered, the "hard bottom with rocks in place" rendered untenable by the incredible revelations of the tectonic geologists.

Once it was enough to assume that, for a period of time, the elements of air and water above, fire below and earth in between conspired to build mountains; then, for a consequent period of time, the elements conspired to tear them down again. But now, with the plate theories of tectonic geology, we take a step back from this local view, and see that both are happening at once everywhere. We have known that the Andes Mountains, for example, are still emerging; but now we are shown that this has less to do with South America than it does with events occurring far off in the middle of the Atlantic and Pacific oceans, where two vast plate-structures growing out of the oceanic rifts are pushing together, the old edge of a Pacific plate sliding under the old edge of an Atlantic plate, tilting the latter up to emerge from the sea in the tidal flats of eastern South America, sloping upward through the great grasslands, rising twenty thousand feet to the crumbling old edge in the clouds above Machu Picchu—one old edge below succumbing to the fire that melts stone, one old edge above succumbing to the water and air that erodes stone: flux above, flux below, and between, a thin interface, resplendent in beauty and terror, that is at least temporarily habitable, capable of harboring an expanding consciousness able to imagine it all.

But where, in this ever-evolving awareness, do we still imagine there might be a hard bottom with rocks in place? A Garden?

> Now a more dismal and fitting day dawns, and a different race
> of creatures awakes to express the meaning of Nature there.

Extremely powerful and momentuous insights into the workings of the world, its life and its Nature, seem to emerge, not as a revelation to one individual, but as a massive manifestation. These moments are articulated by the individuals whose names they come to bear—in the case of the present age, Darwin, Einstein, de Broglie, Heisenberg, Freud . . . but because we have been prepared to listen to what the articulators have to say, because of our growing dissatisfaction with the explanations derived from earlier insights, they are most assuredly and unfortunately our moments, too.

I say unfortunately because, bad as the old explanations might be, they are at least familiar and comfortable, whereas the new, barely-proven and half-explained insights seem to plunge us into unforeseeable turmoil and genuine agony. Nowhere do we see this better than in the fact that our first applications of the insights articulated by Einstein have haunted us with the constant impending threat of extinction. Either we all grow enough to fit the insight, or we will all probably die soon. Only if it works out will we be able to appreciate the symbolic irony.

Hell, we haven't even come to terms with the insights articulated five centuries ago by Copernicus! We have had men sitting on the moon describing the turning of the earth beneath the sun, yet we still say the sun "sets" and the sun also "rises."

Merely a "convention," you will say; and I will agree that probably no more than twenty percent of the people who say "sunrise" and "sunset" *consciously* believe the sun revolves around the earth which sits at the center of the universe. But who, among the other eighty percent, stands still at the bedroom window in the morning and truly senses the tangential rush toward the light? Or are we all in the psychically disoriented state of "knowing" that Copernicus was right but "feeling" that he was basically full of it?

Would it help, say, our children's children, if we replaced "sunrise" and "sunset" with words that implied earth-movement rather than sun-movement? And—the most intriguing question of all—if we came up with those words, would we try to use them, or would we "contend with ourselves," feeling self against knowing self?

Then, once we manage to get ourselves operational in the post-Copernican world, we can begin to try to learn to live intelligently in the post-Darwinian and the post-Einsteinian world. . . .

Obviously, until we learn to incorporate what we "know" into the subconscious roots of our attitudes and feelings, more knowledge won't help us, it will just tear us further apart.

In a book that discusses "higher consciousness" (*The Center of the Cyclone*), "consciousness researcher" John Lilly says that the journey from "orthonoia" (a commonly accepted mind state) to "metonoia" (a new state of consciousness) necessarily leads through paranoia, the derangement and rearrangement of the psyche. That's where the cracks, splits and holes in the floor of the mind are.

"A vast and undeveloped nature which men have not recognized . . . a savage swamp." Welcome to the swamp. Henry wanted to go back a ways, to where the mud didn't look so deep; he wanted to dig down, to see if the Garden isn't there after all . . .

Henry's been down a hundred-and-a-half years now, and still no bottom, no garden. He died, in fact, of a cough and something else he caught in the swamp. But you know what they say about that kind of thing: you can take the monkey out of the jungle, but you can't take the jungle out of the monkey. It's the same with the swamp—you get close to it, it gets close to you. . . .

From the Garden—did you fall, or were you kicked? Like a fledgling ready to fly? It doesn't matter, because here you are, and I can see it in your eyes, the same thing I wondered on first coming here: is the Garden just a memory, or is the Garden just a dream? This swamp: was this the Garden, or is it becoming the Garden? It doesn't matter for now, because it's no Garden now, no hard bottom now; nothing but these floating islands of thrown-together, blown-together reeds and branches and uprooted roots; these drifting things that might be logs or crocagators or something even less useful; a few blackbirds that don't do anything more helpful than sit on the bare branches of water-killed trees and say caw, or are they calling god? . . . They look like they'd like to eat your eyes.

As I see it, we can try to cross. That, of course, assumes there's another side. But crossing is a marginal and tedious-looking proposition in which we are likely to die of unknown causes. Or we can stay here and die of known causes like heart failure and gut erosion. But we can't go back—even now, take just a step or two back . . . that ground you thought was firm on your way here, note the subtle springiness, its slight shifty jelliness, just another floating island—and beneath it the subterranean, subconscious swells of the swamp, the swamp. . . . You can get your mind out of the swamp, but you will never get the swamp out of your mind.

Henry's predilection for the Garden over the "savage swamp" can be easily excused; if he thinks like a pre-Darwinian, it is because he almost is. He and Charles Darwin grew up in the same chronological period; but Henry was the progeny of a civilized agragarian democracy, while Darwin grew up in heathen industrial England, grandson of pioneer scientist Erasmus Darwin, whose legacy was two works (*The Botanic Garden* and *Zoonomia*) that already anticipated evolutionary theory. If Henry and Darwin arrived simultaneously at the edge of the savage swamp, it was as much Henry's heritage to retreat to the Garden (or, rather, to superimpose the Garden) as it was Darwin's to just wade right in, clear-eyed and curious as the Collins's cat.

And there was little doubt at the time as to who carried the day. Darwin set the world on its ear while, even in his own country, Thoreau might as well have talked to the wall. Within a quarter of a century, "evolutionary theory" had been applied and misapplied in every human relationship and inter-relationship in the "natural world," even where it was blatantly out of place. People used Darwin to justify themselves and insult others. Darwin's idea contributed a whole new dimension to human chaos. And Thoreau, with his fastidious pastoral model, hardly created a ripple beyond the bounds of Walden Pond.

But now . . . something else has happened. Call it a counter-revolution—every revolution seems to have one. People discovered that Darwin had not invented a tool to be used for mechanical and social advantage; instead he had created a world picture which, rather than being *used* at all, could only be "accepted." And Thoreau's words, in describing the world-picture of the savage swamp, could not have been more appropriate: if the new picture was more "fitting," it was also, on second glance, much more "dismal." And Einstein! Great god a'mighty, who would thank *him* today?

It seems hardly coincidental that there has been a phenomenal resurrection of interest in tidier models, the old pre-Darwinian worldviews of the great virgin bachelors . . . back to the Bible, back to Jesus, back to

Henry, back to the blooming clockwork Garden, which shines like a beacon, or a burning bush, or tree of knowledge, at the center of a centerless universe. And just in case the old god is dead, as they say in church, we will create a new one, the will of the people, not the will of the shaman-scientist, and we will create, by Act of Congress, a Garden from which we will banish ourselves as anything more than a passing presence, a visitor, until such time as we learn to renounce the temptations of prodigality and pride and come "back to Nature" to move in a natural unchanging harmony. . . .

Recently, David Brower—one of the men largely responsible for the growth and popularization of the "environmental movement" as director of the Sierra Club, and now head of the Friends of the Earth—was asked by the *New York Times* to draw up a set of "operating instructions" for man in his relationship with the environment. His "Operating Instructions for the Third Planet" were printed last year in the *Times* and have since been reprinted elsewhere—in a nice, one-page format, perhaps for cutting out and taping up in a convenient place for constant reference. . . .

Brower begins his piece with what sounds almost like a warranty:

This planet has been delivered wholly assembled and in perfect working condition—

But wait a minute, now—! Let's never mind for the moment that the air-conditioning is totally erratic, making it impossible to predict crops and food supplies from year to year; never mind that on infrequent occasion the heat goes completely erratic, causing great sheets of ice to cover whole continents, or great floods to wash them away; never mind that every now and then an island or a piece of a continent blows up, falls off, or otherwise disappears . . . but what's this that the geologists are telling us today?

They are saying that this planet isn't falling apart at the seams like a Ford, as we've been suspecting. The truth is, it was *never put together at the seams,* but is a fluxion of the aforementioned plates, growing and ceaselessly trying to settle themselves . . . What would you say about your warranty if you took your car into a garage and the mechanic said, "Ah, excellent! See, right here in the fine print—the right front fender is *supposed* to fall off at speeds in excess of fifty. Perfect working condition!"

Brower's "Operating Instructions" include a brief description of "Components": Air, Water, Earth, Life and Fire. About Life, he notes, "Instructions covering the birth, operation and maintenance, and disposal for each living entity have been thoughtfully provided. These instructions are contained in a complex language, called the DNA code, that is not easily understood. However, this does not matter, as the instructions are fully automatic."

This raises again my "Inconceivable Paradox"—how man could be endowed with a creative consciousness and then placed in a circumstance where to use it is extraneous, unnecessary and usually "wrong." Or to put the "Inconceivable Paradox" in Brower's terms, why "thoughtfully" provide instructions if they are neither easily understood nor necessary? And why do something so foreseeably dangerous as put a curious cat like man in proximity to the instructions that, since they aren't necessary for the operation of the planet, can only cause "trouble in the Garden" if unraveled (or, as the case may be, plucked like an apple)?

As for the "Operating Instructions" themselves, Brower is brief and to the point: essentially, don't mess with the components.

It would be ridiculous to assume that David Brower, and most of the people who would accept his "Operating Instructions," don't know about evolution, plate tectonics and the like. Therefore, in trying to jive things like the "Operating Instructions" with the revolution in thinking of the last century (or what should have been a revolution, anyway), I can only conclude that the revolution is ignored because *people don't want it to be true.*

So what we try to·do is keep what we *know* in compartments where it will all remain unrelated and non-coherent—or like the Jackal in *Day of the Jackal,* put that part of ourselves in a suitcase, then throw the suitcase in the river. And in our subconscious selves, where we really live, we let ourselves *believe* in "a planet delivered wholly assembled and in perfect working condition"; a Garden; a Parent Almighty, a "Manufacturer" whose assistance is obtained through repentant prayer; a plan, so that the existential rootless nightmare will ultimately show itself to have been only a fall from grace for violation of the plan, and we will one day wake and return to the flawless and perfectly ordered balance of nature in which all things move harmoniously.

The credo of the "environmental-fundamentalist." I can't poke fun at it, because I have embraced it. But it just doesn't work anymore—not for me anyway. Not under the hard evidence coming in from all parts of the scientific world, and not under the softer, but perhaps more pervasive, experience of four years in the woods. . . .

We are the sons and daughters of Eve and Odin: Eve, who stole the fruit of consciousness and got us banished from the Garden; Odin, whose first conscious act was to slay the great, unconscious source of life. This is a pretty heavy mythic heritage.

We know as a matter of anthropological truth that not all the people on the earth have been so cursed from birth. The American Indian, for example, did not have to begin life by getting kicked out of Paradise; he seemed to belong in the world in which he moved.

Yet whenever we come in contact with a "cyclic" culture in which human nature seems to move in measured harmony with the rest of Nature, the result is the same. We don't just overcome the culture, we absolutely destroy it. And it is always about as easy as falling off a log—as easy as introducing alcohol and smallpox, no trouble at all. We don't even need the rifles, but we carry them in—and the people of those integrated "natural" cultures will war among themselves for the guns, horses, alcohol and small-pox brought by the sons and daughters of Eve and Odin. We are everywhere hated for our success and flattered by imitation. It is a weird goddam mess.

There are two general assumptions we could make about it all. One is pessimistic: that we are degenerative life, cancer, a deathforce. "Bad culture drives out good." The other is not optimistic, is merely "open": that the life, the cyclic cultures, the balance of nature that we might already have altered beyond repair were not the only, or even the best, of all possible worlds. We may not necessarily be worse than what we have destroyed; we may just be something different. And if this is the case, then the future depends, not on the degree to which we can pull back to imitate what we have destroyed, but on our success in learning to exploit that which makes us different.

I grew up in an atmosphere of what I call Walt Disney Anthropomorphism. In my perception of the "natural world," all the animals and plants and everything were just like people, with fur or leaves. In fact, for the most part the animals I was acquainted with—Bambi, Jiminy Cricket, Pogo, Bagheera, Scamper and Company—were better at being people than people were. Things didn't usually get too out of hand until people—we—came into the picture. Eventually the animal-people got things back in order again.

But then I went to the woods.

I remember one snowy day out in the woods—slick and sloppy, but silent—I was riding home from town on my bicycle and I came upon a skunk and a badger maintaining the balance of nature out in an open empty field. I say maintaining the balance of nature; what in fact was happening was that the badger was killing the skunk, and I assume he meant to eat the skunk when he'd finished.

The skunk, of course—pardon his frantic ignorance—didn't get the big picture; and the air was heavy with his only defense. A skunk has a sharp set of teeth, and claws like tenpenny nails, but they are practically useless: his mouth is tiny, his nose in the way, his jaw underslung, and he's as slow and clumsy as a drunken Russian; the awkward assemblage of his frame should be enough to make even the most devoted believer want to ask the great a priori whether the skunk was a dirty trick (on skunks) or just an honest mistake.

The badger seemed totally indifferent to the fact that the skunk was pissing perfume by the liter—cousin to the skunk, the badger is no daisy either, like all the mustelids. In fact, the badger was so indifferent to the smell that he was making his prime target the source of that less than divine odor; although badgers are no speedsters, most anything is faster than a skunk, and the badger was just staying behind the swiveling skunk and playing a very literal and vicious kind of "grab-ass." I suppose there was good badger sense to this particular attack; everywhere else the skunk was covered with thick winter fur, so the badger went for the pink, maybe figuring that in the process of badgering the skunk to death he could take care of half the eating too.

This may sound ridiculous; but it wasn't very funny, or enjoyable; and under the gray, befogged cast of the snowstorm, even though this was nature in the raw—what the adventure films call a life-and-death struggle in the wilds—it wasn't even very interesting. It was, in fact, one of the most boring, tedious, disgusting and offensive exhibitions I have ever watched; and even though it was none of my business, and a typical example of man interfering with "the natural worlds," I broke it up after about twenty minutes with sticks and snowballs and something close to screaming.

The skunk dragged itself right in my direction; passed by me so close I could have reached down and petted it, consoled it . . . but what did I have to say to a skunk trailing blood from both ends, leaving a trail that every predator in the valley would be snurfling down within the day? Buck up, fella—sure it's a hard life, but if we all do our part, it all balances out in the end—*My* end, burbles the skunk through blood, my *ass*. Actually, I don't believe the skunk even saw me. I followed it down to the creek, where it drank the good water through a hole in the ice. Beyond that, I don't know if it survived or not. And what if it did, that day? Tomorrow is another day, and for a skunk what is tomorrow and tomorrow and tomorrow but a long row of badgers, martens, coyotes, badgers, martens, coyotes, and, maybe, the swift, silent, terrible owl?

But leaving the skunk wandering in the willows by the creek, I went back to where I had left my bicycle, now kind of a soft geometry under the accumulating snow. The badger was still at the scene of the *mortuus interruptus,* watching me; it was furious, of course, as I suppose I would be if I were getting ready for a meal and some silly shit came along and took it away. He wasn't frightened of me, not at all—even the badger's little mustelid relative, the weasel, is not afraid of a man; it will take a step toward a man to see if he will retreat, and only then retreat itself, much like a soldier yielding to an unequal field . . . not in fear, but in good sense. I somehow wasn't sorry for the badger, and I frankly didn't care if he starved to death for lack of that meal. Not kind of me, maybe, but for just a moment there, while he was taking my measure, I was off guard and irrationally frightened. Squat, hissing, mean muscle for dull rage and violence. The moment of fear was galvanic to old chemistries. Like some fumbling, paranoid neo-ape for whom the erratic, evolving consciousness was only an impediment to smooth reflexive reactions, I waved a club I didn't have and acted out in superior rage nature's first and most basic form of defense: the bluff.

Unlike Henry, I had no wish to devour this one "for that wildness it represented." And more to the point, I resented—in an uneasy, unarticulated way—the fact that, for all intents and purposes on that gray and ugly afternoon, life in that field had moved on the level of the badger; the badger trundled off and left me the field, yet there was no question as to whose *world* it was out there. My victory was only significant in badger morality.

This reminds me of things I've read and heard about the "sport" of badger-baiting in the "old West." Badger-baiting was a favorite diversion for barbums, second-rate gamblers and the other barbarians of the most powerful family in the animal kingdom, whereby dogs were pushed into battle with a chained badger until the badger was worn out from killing dogs, then took a final, fatal chewing. About all I can say about that, knowing what I know about badgers, barbums and dogs, is that, as a general rule, they probably all deserved one another. And again, the badger wrote the rules. Sure, the badger dies—but can't a badger be a martyr, too? For an animal whose afternoons are usually occupied with eating out of the ass ends of skunks, imagine the fearsome, whirling rush of a day in which he brings a dozen dogs and fifty to two-hundred humanoids into the gray folds of badgerdom, that dull realm of rage and violence! The badger isn't the only thing that dies.

And then, too, there's the cat, the Collins's cat:

> Took to the woods
> Became a wild cat
> Trod in a trap &
> Became a dead cat

A trap set for woodchucks. . . . Somebody, then—probably an Irishman, Thoreau would say—was game for devouring woodchucks for something other than "that wildness they represented."

But what is this trap, what does it represent? An "unnatural perversion"? Not at all. Imagine how the badger might turn green with envy if he could understand this improvement on the art of badgering! Where it would take the badger a good part of the afternoon to run down, dig out and gradually badger a woodchuck to death, man has put his superior mind to work and come up with the trap, so that without his even being present—snap!—as quickly as the owl striking, it is all over. Not necessarily no mess, but certainly no fuss. And if occasionally we get, instead of the woodchuck, a cat or a rat or perhaps the last remaining magnificent bird of kingdom-come, well, we just throw them all behind that bush over there where the other badgers lurk and reset the trap.

But what do we do with the time gained over the badger, who takes half a day for the same work?

We go watch the badger-baiting. Spartacus in the stadium, in the streets, across the seas. And if we occasionally stand up abruptly and, leaving the flickering vicarious struggle, walk to the window and look out; or perhaps even leave the arena in mid-ticket for no particular reason and drive around aimlessly in search of something different, if only a different bar as familiar as the old one is boring . . . we eventually go back, and dismiss (as a praeludium to having to pay off our arena-oriented bets and other second-party commitments, or maybe as just a touch of indigestion) the rising notion that there is *no real reason* why life has to run as though the badger wrote the rules.

Maybe, on occasion, we will even pull all the fighting badgers out of the woods, or out of the Southeast jungle; whereupon we sit for a bit in fidgety, self-congratulatory piety—until we get bored. Then it starts to look as though perhaps the only thing more unbearable than a bad badgerfight is no badgerfight, so we cast about once again for the excuses necessary to rehone the old instincts—making the world safe for this, protecting our interests in that—and reconstruct the operational policies and philosophies that divide the world from the lowest level of life on up into the badgers and the badgered. And we know what happens to the badgered skunk who tries to turn the other cheek.

What are we doing?

We are using that which makes us different to justify acting the same as everything else in the vast eating machine called the balance of nature.

I don't know why we ever came up with that old Walt Disney "Billy Badger and Sammy Skunk" illusion—probably because we so seldom get a chance to see Billy and Sammy as they really are. Or, is it to see Billy and Sammy as *we* really are? . . . only, perhaps, when we aren't aware that we are acting the way *they* really are.

Standing there in that grey and ghostly place in the thick indifferent snow, watching a pissed-off badger walk off one way and the quintessential pissed-on skunk stagger off the other way, unconscious little cogs in the great eating machine, little pork links in the sausage chain of Nature, I could only think: blessed be the unconscious, they know not what they do.

But we do know, or begin to know, a fact that, so far, seems only to manifest itself as kind of a negative grace: consciousness is always having to say we're sorry. Up ahead of me that day were the grey silhouettes of the buildings of Gothic—a few old buildings from a short-lived town dedicated to the extraction of mineral wealth from Nature, but mostly the newer buildings of the summer field station dedicated to the extraction of knowledge from Nature. Conscious knowledge out of the great unconscious, criteria of differentiation out of the immense impending indifference I felt there that day.

We are much concerned today with the study of man's impact on Nature—which we should be. But a chance intrusion of an age-old game of skunks-and-badgers became, for me, a "more dismal and fitting" study of the impact of Nature on man. We display a history as natural as Nature can be: chaotic, indifferent, wild, a culture of eaters and eaten. Practically everything that we call Western Civilization throws the shadow of a badger as big as a dinosaur, feeding on what's left of a skunk that sullenly turns the other cheek because it has no choice, but it longs in its heart to be a bigger badger. . . .

We only seem to transcend this Nature when we imagine "unnatural" re-creations which, unfortunately, never seem to work out as imagined. Our beginnings are full of hope, banners waving in the sun, unveiled models as fine as the finest sand-castle; but then we move out into that "vast and undeveloped nature which men have not recognized," out into the great wood, the swamp, the ocean, the three-in-one of the unconscious, and we find what we thought was our solid beginning to be a reed mat floating away behind us, our destination a mirage that scatters and shimmers and slips away before us, and we begin to grasp at whatever reed realities present themselves. We don't know how to move out consciously into the unconscious, and all the while the unconscious laps at the back of our minds, leaves spider webs in our corners, mouse turds on the butter, the memory of the lonely, distant study in whites and grays of a skunk wandering across a snow-covered hillside, like a period that forgot its sentence. . . .

Whether in our common memories, or dreams, we are brought again and again to the edge of this "savage swamp," the brink of this abyss where we become slowly aware that even the once-solid reality underfoot is but another floating island, and has been all along—larger than most, perhaps, but no less an eventual victim to the subtle eroding undercurrents and sudden boilings-up.

We reject the idea at first, retreating like Henry to look for the "hard bottom" we were so sure was there. Then, cast adrift by the lack of evidence of moorings, we succumb for a while, or forever, to the tides and tempers of the swamp: all is illusion, all is ephemeral, nothing succeeds. There is a kind of cosmic comfort in submission to the unconscious currents that go this way, then that way and, ultimately, go nowhere at all.

It is almost nice, on the one hand, to know that if the unimaginable but oh-too-possible happens and we blow it all apart, it was nothing but a drifting, thrown-together mess of reeds and twigs anyway; nice to be able to go down, finally, relaxed like one accustomed to drowning, to go down thinking, *oh well . . . it wasn't really important anyhow. . . .*

But how much better—isn't it?—to throw one's conscious self into a blazing all-out effort in the ebbing pulse of a deteriorating situation, not to save the situation but to try to transform it, make it once again interesting and alive, setting up the mirrors and running the wires and arranging the sticks and reeds so that, just as the water-logged raft fails to rise from the last swell, the final string is attached, then pulled, and the whole thing rises on wings and moves a little further into the light. . . .

Or so it seemed from where the not-quite-so-young fool sat in the woods, where the spring wells up at the foot of the mountain: thinking, dreaming and fooling around when he should have been hauling home the water, bringing down the wood.

> Such is the character of that morrow which mere lapse of time can never make to dawn. The light which puts out our eyes is darkness to us. Only that day dawns to which we are awake. There is more day to dawn. The sun is but a morning star.
>
> (Henry Thoreau, in concluding his *Life in the Woods*)

Economic Metaphor Redefined: The Transcendental Capitalist at Walden

Judith P. Saunders

Thoreau's thematic and stylistic commitment to paradox manifests itself extravagantly in his persistent efforts to describe his experience at Walden in economic terms. Why would a writer, obviously attuned to the derivative and connotative meanings of words, choose to convey the joys of a *natural* and spiritual life with the language of business and commerce? With a seemingly naive disregard for the inappropriate, Thoreau discusses his "accounts," his "ventures," or his "industry," carefully calculating such factors as "cost," "interest," and "capital." Availing himself at every conceivable opportunity of images and vocabulary with commercial connotations, he creates what Stanley Cavell [in *The Senses of Walden*] has called "parodies of American means of evaluation." Shrewdly he exposes the insidious control exerted over our lives by the economic system of profit and loss which we so easily take for granted.

There is no doubt where Thoreau stands in the confrontation between spiritual and material values. He tells us that "trade curses every thing it handles," and he chastises the farmer who abuses his fields, "measuring them by the dollar only." Trade and money are unequivocally depreciated as measures of worth. "I respect not his labors, his farm where every thing has its price; who would carry the landscape, who would carry his God, to market, if he could get anything for him." In this passage from "The Ponds," Thoreau contrasts the miserly legal owner of the land with persons like himself, whose love and enjoyment of it are not profit-oriented. He

From *American Transcendental Quarterly* 36 (Fall 1977). © 1977 by Kenneth Walter Cameron.

plays off multiple meanings dazzlingly, noting that any unsaleable aspect of the landscape is worthless to the farmer: "there was nothing to redeem it, forsooth, in his eyes." In the word "redeem" we hear both economic and religious reverberations. Combining the values of a pawnbroker with those of a preacher, the farmer reveals that for him monetary and religious "redemption" are one and the same. Speaking of this same farmer, Thoreau notes, "it was no *privilege* to him to behold [the landscape]," i.e., he does not exercise the real and inherent "privilege," or advantage, of living on the land, but merely holds his legal "privilege," or title. On this man's farm "nothing grows free": nothing grows unconstrained and unregulated because nothing is without its price.

Given this bias against commercial valuation, as opposed to other, nonmaterialistic kinds of valuation, we are forced to ask why Thoreau should use the vocabulary of a Yankee capitalist so abundantly, and with such apparent innocence in *Walden*. Of course, he is not alone in his propensity to discuss matters of the mind and spirit in quantitative terms. Carlyle, for instance, had already exploited some of the ironic possibilities of such a vocabulary switch in *Sartor Resartus* (1833–34). In the well-known chapter concerning "The Everlasting Yea" he speaks of human happiness in financial images: overplus, deficit, payment, wages, fund. He offers a formula for happiness as one might offer a geometric proof: "The Fraction of Life can be increased in value not so much by increasing your Numerator as by lessening your Denominator." The sarcasm of such metaphor is harsh, and Carlyle is quick to deprecate contemporary "shallow superficial faculties . . . Arithmetical Understanding," and "Profit-and-loss Philosophy." Leaving aside the very real differences between Carlyle's use of economic imagery and Thoreau's, there remains a strikingly similar reversal of eighteenth-century rationalism in the prose of these two nineteenth-century romantic writers. Cherished concepts of the Age of Reason—the world as a machine, God the Watchmaker, scientific method—are unceremoniously pushed to ludicrous extremes. The real question is whether the precision and irrefutability of the exact sciences can ever, in all earnestness, be applied to intuitive and subjective experience. Along with some of his contemporaries, Thoreau utilizes the vocabulary and methods of scientific exactitude to raise this fundamental romantic question, and he comes up with his own typically unique answers.

His choice of economic imagery very precisely demonstrates how overwhelmingly our vision of life is dominated by commercial values. Our language seems riddled with economic implications. "I did not wish to live what was not life, living is so dear," he writes, confronting us with the rather embarrassing semantic fact that we tend to confuse what is costly, or expensive, with what is precious in the noncommercial sense. "I think that we may safely trust a good deal more than we do. We may waive just so much care of ourselves as we honestly bestow elsewhere." He exploits multiple meanings in the concept of *trusting,* and creates an image of life, or selfhood, as a measurable commodity to be "waived" or "bestowed," as in a business transaction. The puns on such words as interest, account, employ, improve, spend, save (as Cavell indicates, the list is interminable), point remorselessly to the financial frame of reference which governs our thought processes, our value system, and our very language. We are prisoners of capitalist ideology, and cannot without thought and determined effort escape the concepts which have infiltrated our vocabulary. The way of escape Thoreau proposes in his puns involves returning to a pre-capitalist definition of terms. The *OED* confirms that a surprising number of the words in question (e.g., privilege, free, dear) did not always have specifically economic meanings. "Prospect" meant view, or lookout, and only later acquired the additional meaning of worldly expectations; "dear" meant rare and glorious before it means expensive; "profit" meant improvement or advantage in the general sense before it acquired a specifically commercial sense; "fortune" meant chance or luck before it meant wealth. Where we go wrong is in thinking that advantage (profit) must be material, that preciousness (dearness) is chiefly monetary, or that luck (fortune) always involves financial well-being. Thoreau seems to suggest that we can rescue our understanding of these terms and restore their original sense—a sense which implicitly includes economic meanings, but within a much broader context. Disconcertingly, he remarks, "I see young men, my townsmen, whose misfortune it is to have inherited farms, houses, barns, cattle." In Thoreau's scheme of things, to inherit goods and property is a *"mis*fortune" in the older, primary meaning of bad luck. His townsmen's fortunes are their misfortune, and the materialistic definition of "fortune" is put to shame by Thoreau's larger and more inclusive definition. The paradox in his remark is resolved when we revise our purely economic view of the world. By ironic manipulation of multiple response, Thoreau expands and restores the potential of our vocabulary; he opens the way for words to *mean more,* and therefore to describe our experience in terms other than the merely commercial and mathematical.

A familiar passage from "The Ponds" displays Thoreau's virtuosity at packing his sentences with economically oriented vocabulary. There were, he claims, "days when idleness was the most attractive and productive industry. Many a forenoon have I stolen away, preferring to spend thus the most valued part of the day; for I was rich, if not in money, in sunny hours and summer days, and spent them lavishly; nor do I regret that I did not waste more of them in the workshop or the teacher's desk." The obstinately paradoxical equation of "idleness" with "industry" challenges from the outset our usual linguistic responses. We can make sense of Thoreau's statement only by rethinking concepts like "idleness," "productive," or "industry," and by shifting meanings away from property and material interest. (Must one turn out marketable goods in order to be "productive"? Need "industry" inevitably be characterized by concrete, material results of labor?) A similar value shift occurs in the other key phrases, which play more obviously on multiple possibilities for meaning: stolen away, spend, most valued part, spent them lavishly, waste. Any one of these phrases might seem innocent enough standing alone, but by placing them in such close proximity Thoreau creates a world controlled by financial meanings and values. We are compelled to read "forenoon" as the object of the verb phrase "to steal away": time not spent increasing wealth is "stolen," and time itself is a kind of property which Thoreau must take from himself. The word "spend" continues to equate time with money, while the phrase "most valued part" asks the more fundamental question: Of what does value consist? "I was rich" makes explicit the gap between wealth in the Thoreauvian sense and wealth in the commercial sense. Having fought our way through a passage thus laden with deliberately planned double meanings, we can no longer approach words like "spend" or "waste" or "rich" with our old naivete. Our materialistic orientation to language and to the world stands condemned and corrected.

Besides demonstrating that there is, indeed, a world beyond the commercial one, Thoreau slyly turns the tables on his audience by making a virtue of business methods. In his opening remarks he announces his intention of writing "an account" of his life, likewise demanding a "simple and sincere account" from other writers, and so sets up the implied comparison with business and bookkeeping which operates quietly throughout *Walden*. He is careful to include meticulous accounts in his "account," assuring us that one of his chief purposes in writing is to recommend a practical and *economical* mode of living. The overlapping meanings define his belief that he must account for his life in the same way that a bookkeeper must account for funds. "Life" consists of a limited amount of time and energy, which may be conserved, saved, spent, employed, squandered, or hoarded—just like property. Thoreau suggests that if we must think of life in economic terms, we might at least apply decent economic principles to its management. In "Sounds" he speaks of mornings spent in revery instead of hoeing beans: "They were not time subtracted from my life, but so much over and above my usual allowance." This metaphor explicitly equates "life" with an allotment of time, each person presumably having a portion rationed out to him. The phrases "subtracted from," "over and above," and "usual allowance" draw a parallel between "life" and the records from an army supply unit. Similarly, when Thoreau declares in the same paragraph, "I love a broad margin to my life," he is making obvious metaphoric reference to the economic sense of the word (margin of profit) as well as to the graphical sense (margin of a book) and to the ordinary sense (margin of safety). He is talking of his life quite literally as if it were an account of an "allowed" income, to be added to or subtracted from, with a margin of profit at stake. He gives a mathematical accounting of his occupations and possessions as well as a moral and metaphysical accounting, or answering, for them.

In comparing his life (and his book) to a financial record, Thoreau is taking his audience's capitalist ideology to its logical conclusion. He is being as careful with his life as his neighbors are with their possessions. Along with the sarcasm evident in his description of life as something mathematically measureable, or the experiment at Walden as "trade . . . with the Celestial Empire," there is a real commitment to the methods of commerce, if not to its ends. "I have always endeavored to acquire strict business habits; they are indispensable to every man." "What recommends commerce to me is its enterprise and bravery." "Commerce unexpectedly confident and serene, alert, adventurous, unwearied. It is very *natural* in its methods withal." In defining commerce as a natural activity, he overcomes the disparity we assume (and hence create) between natural processes and human institutions. In his own peculiar way he turns out to be perhaps the shrewdest Yankee capitalist of all. The good businessman is responsible, attentive, *accountable*. He keeps careful records; he knows what comes in and what goes out. He is bold, energetic, ingenious; he takes risks. He is industrious and enterprising in the best and broadest sense. Certainly these are all traits which Thoreau recommends to anyone wanting to strike out for the life of transcendental self-discovery. Encouraging us to make "good ventures," he frees the concept of "venturing" from its restrictive, financial interpretation; similarly, he frees us from our bondage to commercial interest by showing us how the virtues we have misapplied may be used to far better purpose. This is the ultimate point of the extended analogy between his life at Walden and trading with the Celestial Empire. As he painstakingly enumerates the similarities between his neighbors' enterprises and his own, he dramatically expands our definition of "good business."

Perhaps the most distinctive trait of the good businessman is his concern for comparative value. His priorities must be well defined. And is this not Thoreau's chief concern as well? In order to avoid living "what [is] not life" (since "living is so *dear*"), he determines what it is that has most value and meaning for him—and then changes his life accordingly. Where Thoreau quarrels with the capitalist businessman is not in the businessman's determination to get and keep what he wants, but rather in his decisions about what things are worth wanting. "We are often reminded that if there were bestowed on us the wealth of Croesus, our aims must still be the same, and our means essentially the same." The pun on "means" emphasizes that the methods necessary to good business are the same ones necessary to good living, and that the resources available to us are not primarily financial. Our ways and means, our energy and industry, are not bad, they are simply misdirected. Investing and venturing, improving and accounting, spending and saving, are psychologically and socially necessary. Our mistake is in treating our property and possessions with more care than we take of our lives. Thoreau is serious about living according to economic principles of profit and loss: he stops eating fish because catching and cleaning them is too much trouble and "cost more than it came to." Defining "the cost of a thing" as "the amount of what I will call life which is required to be exchanged for it," he has brilliantly inverted the values behind our economic principles, making life—instead of property—the highest good. He earnestly advises us to "mind our business" as well as we possibly can, but first we have to establish what our real business in life *is*. In short, Thoreau would have us learn to be far more economical than we are at present.

In readjusting our conception of economy, we find ourselves encroaching upon the territory of sacred tradition. One function of the all-pervasive economic metaphor in *Walden* is to remind us of another important book in which such metaphor abounds. Cavell discusses Thoreau's "brutal mocking of our sense of values, by forcing a finger of the New Testament (hence of our understanding of it) down our throats. For that is the obvious origin or locus of the use of economic imagery to express, and correct, spiritual confusion: What shall it profit a man; the wages of sin; the parable of talents; laying up treasures; rendering unto Caesar; charity." The description of the divine in terms of the secular is a basic rhetorical technique in the New Testament. Wholly accustomed to business imagery in the religious context, we easily forget that it is, after all, figurative language. The phrase "kingdom of heaven" is to most people a dead metaphor; describing the next life in terms of political and economic power structures appropriate to this life has through repetition lost the shock value it once had. Thoreau tries to restore some of this lost shock effect by grossly exaggerating the invasion of economic imagery into spiritual matters. Calvinist New England had always tended to overemphasize the economic implications of the New Testament and to interpret them in an appallingly literal sense. In *Walden* the earthly kingdom exercises such metaphoric control over the heavenly kingdom that we reach the point of hyperbole. Thoreau is determined to hoist us with our own petard, and he sets about it with great gusto.

He recasts biblical imagery to show New England bibliolaters their mistake: applying a business ethic to matters of faith, they have thrown out Christian doctrine in order to worship Christian metaphor. His insistent reiteration of such terms as profit and loss, advantage and gain, interest and prospects, is meant to generate new awareness. He criticizes, for example, the "pathetically wise" and "prudent landlord" who takes so much trouble to cut and store Walden ice, anticipating in January "the heat and thirst of July. . . . It may be that he lays up no treasures in this world which will cool his summer drink in the next." This remark seems deliberately to contradict the injunction of Matthew: "Lay not up for yourselves treasures upon earth, where moth and rust doth corrupt, and where thieves break through and steal" (6:19). But both Matthew and Thoreau are rebuking our tendency to accumulate material comforts and ignore spiritual welfare. Where they differ is in their use of the word "treasures." Matthew uses the word in the specifically materialistic, monetary sense: "treasures" means *material wealth.* Thoreau, however, forces us to define the concept in a much broader context: "treasures" means *things of real value.* In Thoreau's sentence we must recognize that value—preciousness—is also measurable in nonmaterial terms, and that the kind of treasures Matthew warns us against are not really valuable in this world any more than they are in the next. Matthew focuses on a negative commandment; he tells us what not to do and what not to want. Thoreau emphasizes the positive side of the question: spiritual growth is precious. It is *treasure,* treasure we can lay up right now in this life. He makes it seem easy to do what is spiritually valuable, while Matthew makes it seem difficult. "Lay not up for yourselves treasures" sounds like renunciation, but Thoreau tells us we are giving up *true* "treasures" right now in favor of less valuable things. Do lay up treasures for yourselves, he urges, and so turns renunciation into fulfillment. By a simple expansion of vocabulary he transcends Matthew's psychological negativism. The potential danger of such biblical imagery as "treasures," "profit," and the like, is that it encourages us to cherish money and property as the highest values. By all manner of subtle alteration and irreverent hyperbole

Thoreau pushes us to see the metaphor *as metaphor,* and so frees us to return to the underlying scriptural truth. Christ had asked, "Wist ye not that I must be about my Father's business?" (Luke 2:49). Having scraped the barnacle of dead metaphor from our religious perceptions, Thoreau echoes Christ with deliberate emphasis: "If we are alive, let us go about our business." We are persuaded by now that our chief "business" is not commercial, any more than the best "treasures" lie in bank vaults.

Thoreau continues to expose our emphasis on ownership for what it is (a secular sacrament) by pushing it to ludicrous extremes. Talking of the bare strip of shore created around Walden Pond by changes in water level, he remarks, "By this fluctuation the pond asserts its title to a shore, and . . . the trees cannot hold it by right of possession." Even if we have forgotten how out of keeping it is to speak of the "kingdom" of God or the "redemption" of sin, this image forces us to realize how our business mania has distorted our view of the world. The idea of a body of water "asserting its title," or trees maintaining their "right of possession" is more than merely inappropriate; it is grotesquely absurd. The absurdity stands as a reproach against our confusion of values; it calls into question the whole notion of ownership. How can a pond "own" its shore? What does it mean to say that a tree "possesses" the ground it grows on? By the irrationality evident in such misplaced economic terminology, Thoreau generates uncertainty in our minds about the most fundamental principle of capitalism. Ownership is a superstition, an act of faith; it does not correspond to any empirically observable reality. This is the message of Thoreau's economic hyperbole. As he shows us how our possession-oriented thinking must end, the very trees and ponds turn capitalist.

We have relegated even God himself to membership in the economic establishment. Thoreau notes the pervasiveness of the leaf design throughout creation, and exclaims with apparent naivete: "Thus it seemed that this one hillside illustrated the principle of all the operations of Nature. The Maker of this earth but patented a leaf." His mood here is expansive and joyful, but still he cannot resist taking a slap at his audience's capitalist imperative. Even more preposterous is the mixing of ecstasy and sarcasm in this encomium to Walden: "Successive nations perchance have drank at, admired, and fathomed it, and passed away, and still its water is green and pellucid as ever. . . . Perhaps on that spring morning when Adam and Eve were driven out of Eden Walden Pond was already in existence. . . . Even then it had . . . obtained a patent of heaven to be the only Walden Pond in the world and distiller of celestial dews." The head-on conflict between Christian vocabulary (Adam and Eve, Eden, heaven, celestial) and business practice (obtained a patent, distiller) simply will not be ignored. To define Walden's unique and everlasting beauty by turning heaven into a patent office is to reestablish the *metaphoric* nature of biblical language. Thoreau's ludicrous talk of patents and titles suggests to even the dullest reader that such scriptural terms as "profit," "gain," and "treasure" are not meant to be taken literally. New England Calvinist interpretations of Christianity are based on false linguistic assumptions, which Thoreau's exaggerated metaphor corrects. Ownership itself appears ever more bizarre and incomprehensible when even identity ("to be the only Walden Pond in the world") becomes a matter of legal title. It is Thoreau's mission to ridicule and undermine our belief in this, the last mystery and doctrine remaining in a presumably scientific age. With apparent wrongheadedness, he persistently applies the vocabulary of possession to precisely those things which by definition can never be owned. Things worth having (e.g., the landscape, sunny hours, and summer days) are not transferable. A tree needs no title to the space it occupies, and even a pauper "owns" his afternoons in a sense that transcends legal right. These are natural and inevitable relationships which cannot be affected in any real way by legal mumbo jumbo concerning deeds and titles. Even if I am compelled to "spend" my afternoons "digging in this dirt," they are still indisputably *mine*. This is exactly what Thoreau intends us to realize: it would seem sensible to take care of what is naturally and inalienably ours before we begin to fuss about portable property. The thrust of Thoreau's reversal of terms is toward a radical reversal of priorities.

Ultimately the persuasive power of his economic theorizing derives from the deliberate paradox of his rhetorical approach to his subject—his use of commercial language to undermine our commitment to commerce. His manipulation of language teaches us that most of the economic principles we take for granted can be rescued by redefining the key concept of "value." Shifting our system onto a new ground structure, he has subverted its aims without destroying its methods. By the language he chooses to convey his experience, Thoreau defies us to deny that he is more economical in his mode of living than we. He demands and gets top value, and never pays more for a thing than it is worth. And though he claims "to speak impartially . . . and as one not interested in the success or failure of the present economical and social arrangements," it is clear that his investments are bringing in better returns than ours. The "present . . . arrangements" are a failure even in their own terms.

"A True Integrity Day by Day": Thoreau's Organic Economy in *Walden*

Harold Hellenbrand

> *I hesitate to say these things, but it is not because of the subject,—I care not how obscene my words are,—but because I cannot speak them without betraying my impurity.*
>
> Henry David Thoreau

Certainly, it is no secret that Thoreau's *Walden* concerns spending. "To discover how to earn and spend our wakeful hours—whatever we are doing—is the task of *Walden* as a whole," writes Stanley Cavell [in *The Senses of Walden*]. Economic terms such as "spend," "account," "business," and "transact" recur throughout the text. They abound especially in the first chapter, "Economy." But Thoreau does not permit these terms to rest drowsily in a context of financial loss and gain. Rather, he wakes them, makes them metaphors for forgotten spiritual and organic values. He subverts both the business ethic and the dull round of language itself. Each economic word contains within it an alarm of meaning that prevents us from falling into a sleepy discourse with the surface of the text.

What are the values, specifically, that disrupt the common sense of economic language and threaten to rouse the reader? To call them moral or spiritual is to describe them vaguely; to say that they are "Christian doctrine," in an effort to suggest the resonance of Thoreau's lessons with Matthew's injunctions against laying up the treasures of this world, is perhaps misleading. After all, does not Thoreau often subvert and awaken

From *ESQ: A Journal of the American Renaissance* 25, no. 2 (1979). © 1979 by Harold Hellenbrand.

biblical metaphors, much as he challenges the language of business? For Thoreau, "economy" and hence the words that come under its heading mean complexly. If *Walden* is about spending money and spending time, it also concerns building a cottage and nourishing a body and tending a mind. The very word "economy" connotes managing household, body, mind, and spirit. Not until we see how radically consubstantial Thoreau's project was in *Walden,* how he insisted on the confluence of habitation, body, and soul, can we approach an understanding of his economy.

Thoreau suggested that, symbolically, a man's clothing differed little from his dwelling. Both were outer garments of the soul, but neither was "exogenous." One should be able to lay a hand on the boards of a person's house and feel beneath them rippling muscles and swelling veins, just as a shirt should not shelter the skin from the touch. Clothing and housing were the insulating layers of a vital economy. "According to Liebig, man's body is a stove, and food the fuel which keeps up the internal combustion in the lungs. . . . The animal heat is the result of a slow combustion, and disease and death take place when this is too rapid." Maintaining a degree of heat prosperous for body and soul, this was a matter primarily of biological, not financial, economy. If the "stove" was too well covered in clothes and boards, or if the fueling food was too rich, then the human product was unfortunately overcooked. "The luxuriously rich are not simply kept comfortably warm, but unnaturally hot; as I implied before, they are cooked, of course *à la mode.*" Implicitly, an extravagant person roasted, dished, and cannibalized himself. Or, in the terms of another metaphor, he transformed himself into a "machine" and a tool of his tools since he made his body into a virtual stove that did little more than process food and wear itself down.

For the human stove to function properly, for it to sublimate matter into soul and not just waste its fuel, its keeper had to blend the nature outside his body with the nature within. He had to make of his life and environment "a true integrity." The chronology of Thoreau's cabin-building reflected this philosophy. In the beginning of the spring, 1845, Thoreau ventured out to Walden and commenced chopping pine for his home. In May, he raised a frame out of this wood. After hoeing in the fall, he built a chimney "before a fire became necessary for warmth," and by winter he shingled the sides of the cabin. Building followed the necessity of the seasons. Never was there more wooden garment than body needed. Thus always could Thoreau "feel the influence of the spring of springs," the imperative within nature calling him to "a higher and more ethereal life." Evidently, what Thoreau called "ethereal life" could not be produced ar-

orates and inspires us." Human nature was hard to overcome, Thoreau observed; but it had to be subdued if the spirit was to flower.

To think that Thoreau advocated a monkish asceticism, castigating all the pleasures of this world, is, of course, to misunderstand him. His conception of economy bound him organically to nature; he was part of its system of exchange, its currency. The supply that had to be taken into account was nature's, and the demand that had to be answered was human nature's. By no means did he propose an otherworldly exclusiveness. But Thoreau did feel that only the person in whom the "animal" was dying out could achieve blessedness. Blessedness was the fruit of what Thoreau, tongue-in-cheek, called the " 'bran new' theory of life."

Thoreau intended to starve the "animal" in himself. He would not consume meat. Meat was a fuel too rich; meat was "unclean." It congested his "stove," causing stomach and lungs to work too hard. Also, since meat was expensive, the human carnivore had to devote an inordinate amount of time and money to procuring it. If he owned livestock, then he found himself, somewhat absurdly, slaving to feed his own four-legged dinners. Meat was not the only victim of Thoreau's dietetic putsch. Salt and spices had to go, for they tended to make fueling the body a luxury, an end in itself. Body and imagination "should both sit down at the same table." Thus, diet was as symbolic as it was practical. Thoreau observed that a Puritan could attack his meager "brown-bread crust" with the rapaciousness of a carnivore. Proper diet consisted as much in one's "devotion" to food as in the food consumed. Vegetarianism did not, as a matter of course, confer sainthood.

While he avoided meat, Thoreau did not plan to make his diet less wild. He did intend to make himself more "humane." Was not his bean-field a hybrid of forest and farm? Did it not represent the wild cultured barely? In the beginning of "Higher Laws," Thoreau acknowledged two impulses within his breast, one for the wild and one for the spiritual. There were times when he yearned to sink his teeth into a woodchuck "and devour him raw; not that I was hungry then, except for that wildness which he represented." Also were there times when Thoreau wandered through the woods, "like a half-starved hound, with a strange abandonment, seeking some kind of venison which I might devour." This wildness Thoreau reverenced especially when, in a mind less abandoned and less hound-like, a mind more human and humane, he could harness the impulse. The wood-chopper who visited him occasionally was "a great consumer of meat" and not inhuman at all for his diet. His strenuous life demanded pails of cold woodchuck for replenishment. Still, although the woodchopper could explain the principles of exchange and barter more clearly than most philosophers, he had not matured past the stage of "the animal man." "The intellectual and what is called spiritual man in him were slumbering as in an infant." The woodchopper rested contentedly on the first plateau of dietetic economy and mental life.

The woodchopper's active profession, the facts that he labored with his hands and was, in a beneficent sense, "cousin to the pine and the rock," justified his eating habits. He had as much right to consume meat as any other of nature's wild creatures. For civilized and socialized humans, for people who did not labor so strenuously or who sweated needlessly in unnatural vocations, there was no excuse for carnivorousness. In fact, meat-eating symbolized the hypocrisy of their lives; it epitomized and reinforced their sophisticated brutality.

In "The Bean-Field" Thoreau set out to describe the peaceable art of hoeing. Suddenly he interrupted his narrative. He turned eastward to Concord and punctured his pastoral mood, much as the train intruded into the felicitous musings of "Sounds." He said that some days he "had a vague sense . . . of some sort of itching and disease in the horizon, as if some eruption would break out there soon, either scarlatina or canker-rash." From Concord the rhythms of patriotic music wafted through the woods and reached his ears. The marital cadences inspired him to think that he "could spit a Mexican with a good relish,—for why should we always stand for trifles?" He "looked round for a woodchuck or a skunk to exercise my chivalry upon." Bitterly, he associated cannibalism with his own nation's attempt to ingest its southern neighbor in the Mexican War. Dietetic and political metaphors converged and signaled once more Thoreau's complex sense of economy. He implied that a nation's political life could be no purer than the sum of its citizens' personal economies, their diets, financial expenditures, and social regimens. In "Higher Laws" Thoreau reflected that the "vast abdomens" of "nations without fancy and imagination" betray their grossness. Did he have in mind then, as he did in "The Bean-Field," the ever-widening girth of America's underbelly in the Southwest?

Thoreau's ideal economy was a closed and replete one, a cycle of energy that replenished itself seasonally. While he decided not to eat animal food, he also refused to introduce animal manure into his bean-field. His farming would lose its integrity if it was nurtured by an animal other than himself. Manure, like meat, was alien really to his vegetable habitat. Perhaps it also reminded him of the animal impurities that threatened to clog his body's economy and strain his breathing; he wanted to avoid even indirect contamination. Philosophically, Thoreau's intention to bring only himself, tools, seeds, and a few incidentals to Walden made sense. After all, Walden was a venture in self-sufficiency, and his agriculture would have to reflect its ingenuity and simplicity.

Still, Thoreau's fields needed fertilizing. This fact he could not ignore in his agriculture, nor did he ignore it in *Walden*. Michael West has read in Thoreau's allusions to "squatting" and "sitting" in fields puns on defecating. Thoreau deposited rather natural claims on the land. Land was his only insofar as he contributed to its culture. Indeed, Thoreau called himself a "squatter." Since he did not consume meat, or consumed it only rarely, his body's waste was a product of the fields themselves. His economy, his exchange with nature, was vegetable.

The nourishment with which Thoreau's fecal economy enriched the land was matched by nature's own vegetable fecundity. Old stumps of wood that Thoreau removed from the land fed the fire in his cabin admirably; and the mold left by the stumps fertilized the soil, feeding the food that Thoreau would later prepare over the fire in his cabin. In a sense, wood was the special coinage of *Walden*. The labor involved in moving it from field to hearth was highly productive; accumulating it enriched the fields and Thoreau's own cabin. As a currency, however, wood symbolized what was potentially worst in money, the waste of time and labor. These implications Thoreau filled out in "House-Warming."

From a psychological point of view, "House-Warming" was a crucial chapter in *Walden*. Winter enveloped the pond, and the cold forced solitude on Thoreau. Could he survive aloneness? Could he so manage body and home to imbibe, even in the dead of winter, what vitalizing sustenance there was outside of his woods and cloth shells? "I withdraw yet further into my shell and endeavored to keep a bright fire within my house and within my breast," Thoreau reported. To compensate for the cold outside, he increased his consumption of wood, and he searched for the richest wood that he could find. In the "stove" metaphor of "Economy," Thoreau had implied that wood was a symbol for food and that rich food strained the body's bellows, its lungs. But the coldness, the reality of nature's seasonal hostility, led Thoreau to ignore this tenet of moderate economy. In winter, Thoreau observed, every man accumulated wood to keep his home warm, and everyone gazed "at his wood-pile with a kind of affection." Accumultion was a universal activity: it represented labor achieved and promised comfort. Wise foresters, like Thoreau, knew that "fat pine roots," buried where stumps had been excavated, were a special luxury. "A few pieces of fat pine were a great treasure" because they burned so well. "With axe and shovel you explore this mine, and follow the marrowy store, yellow as

beef tallow, or as if you had struck on a vein of gold, deep into the earth."
Words such as "fat," "beef tallow," and "gold" suggested that this wood—
or rather the comfort that it promised—contained within it the root of evil.
Gold was no part of Thoreau's commerce with the Celestial Empire; and
beef tallow certainly was not part of his dietary economy. Something was
amiss in "House-Warming."

One winter afternoon, Thoreau left his cabin with a fire burning in
the hearth. "It was I and Fire that lived there" in the cabin, Thoreau commented, domesticating and personifying fire. Suddenly, in the woods the
urge overcame him to look back at his dwelling. Perhaps, he feared, Fire
had gotten out of hand. Sure enough, "I looked and saw that a spark had
caught my bed, and I went in and extinguished it when it had burned a
place as big as my hand." Fire, bed, and hand. The sexual implications of
the words, grouped together, intruded into Thoreau's rather calm narration
of how he averted disaster narrowly. The fire in the hearth and the fire that
escaped the hearth represented Thoreau's own "animal life," for he had
analogized his own body with a "stove." Cryptically, Thoreau alluded to
masturbating. The rich wood that his fireplace ingested, the beef and gold
that he feared consuming, led to the energetic depletion that the coughing
and hissing train symbolized in "Sounds." But in "House-Warming" the
depletion was sexual, not respiratory. Thoreau undermined the cult of
domesticity, of comfort and warmth, by suggesting its economic depravity
even as he revealed the sexual hazards of his own solitude.

The masturbation passage was a crucial one in *Walden*, for it domesticated the lesson of the locomotive. Dissipation was as much a hazard of
household and body as it was of commerce and industry. Masturbation
was Thoreau's only excrementitious act in *Walden*. His feces were not really
waste since they nourished his "sedes," his plot. They served a higher end.
Masturbation served no such end. Thoreau's allusion to it was not gratu-
itous; the passage followed logically from the pattern of *Walden*'s imagery.
Always Thoreau prided himself on "the labor of his hands." He built his
own cabin, hoed his own fields, and notched his own pen. He philosophized
that most men's "fingers, from excessive toil, are too clumsy and tremble
too much" to pluck life's "finer fruits." Hands were the agents of Thoreau's
economy as feet were the roots to the subsoil of nutriment. "My head is
hands and feet," Thoreau reflected. Ideally, hands were subordinate to head,
for in the head were Thoreau's "highest faculties." He took supreme pleasure in the exercise of the intellect, in reading, thinking, and farming. "I
do not wish to be any more busy with my hands than is necessary," he
said. Hands, though, could escape the head's supervision occasionally, and

when they did, they acted the villain. In masturbation, in which they were the culprits ("a place as big as my hand"), they sinned. But the sin was not in masturbation itself as an affront to morality and religion. What was sinful was the expense of spirit, labor, and time.

Masturbation was an occupational hazard of Emersonian man; so was promiscuity. Emersonian man, and Thoreau as a disciple, walked a thin line between depletion in society and in his own home. Self-help handbooks of the mid-nineteenth century tolled the dangers of "effundendi manu" or releasing the body's spirits through the hands. In a period of despair, Emerson wrote in language [in "Experience"] that is rather difficult to explain away: "I take this evanescence and lubricity of all objects, which lets them slip through our fingers then when we clutch hardest, to be the most unhandsome part of our condition." Surely this description of the "unhandsome" relied on the imagery of masturbation to dramatize its feelings of despair, loneliness, and waste.

Thoreau's vegetarian diet for avoiding excessive stimulation and thus various types of depletion, such as masturbation, was an old remedy. Since at least the eighteenth century physicians had identified spices such as salt, stimulants such as coffee, and staples such as meat as fuels of masturbation, when consumed in abundance. Food, however, was not the only dangerous indulgence. Catherine Beecher warned her readers of the hazards of "highly wrought fictions" for the solitary and young mind. John Todd, an advice manualist, inveighed in a chapter entitled "Reading" against the dangers of masturbation. He feared that prurient and even suspenseful literature could excite a reader to begin "building castles in the air," to fantasize. And fantasy, because reality could never meet its expectations, led inevitably to unfortunate self-indulgences.

"If you have built castles in the air, your work need not be lost; that is where they should be. Now put the foundations under them," wrote Thoreau in a buoyant mood in *Walden*. But was he always confident that at Walden Pond he was actually incorporating himself into a replete and healthy economy? Could not the entire scheme of fronting the facts of nature, alone, be mad—a castle with no foundations, a head and hands with no feet? The theme of insanity and its implications for the diverse but organically related meanings of economy in *Walden* cannot be ignored; Thoreau did not ignore them in "Solitude."

Like the loon who retreated to "solitary ponds" in moulting season, Thoreau ventured to Walden to continue his metamorphosis into a more natural and spiritual creature. The loon was a discomforting and paradoxical symbol. Certainly the bird was a figure of metamorphosis, of moulting and self-transcendence, but it also exemplified the extremes of psychic experience as it soared into the sky and plunged beneath the surface of the pond. The bird's "demoniac laughter" seemed to mock Thoreau when he chased it across the waters of Walden. Was the Walden project merely a "loon" chase? Or did the bird symbolize and articulate in its sounds some meaning lurking in the pond and thus in Thoreau's venture to it? If the venture was insane, or if at least in moments of despair Thoreau considered it so, then the masturbation passage in "House-Warming" assumes added significance. It was not unusual to link insanity—castle-building—and self-indulgence, specifically masturbation. The fire run amok in Thoreau's cabin dramatized his self-doubt, his fear that in solitude he was losing his sanity and the healthful economy that he ventured to Walden to achieve in the first place. Perhaps Thoreau's domestic personification of Fire expressed his longing for the reinforcement of company.

Despite momentary fears of insanity and dissipation, *Walden* was largely the record of successful economy and sublimation. The book itself, as the product and "account" of the experiment, would seem to justify Thoreau's choice to lead a frontier existence. But we must adjust our notions of ends and means to Thoreau's philosophy. He insisted on the radical and instantaneous dependence of his culture on his agriculture. In other words, *Walden,* his end, was implicit in his survival at Walden, his means. The density of his language, the meanings that he compacted into economy, expressed his desire to fuse together the commercial, political, and dietetic activities of human life. Truly, Thoreau's intent was to live and to describe "a true integrity day by day."

Few passages in *Walden* expressed Thoreau's integrity as succinctly as his description of hoeing in "The Bean-Field." While the bean-field was ripe for cultivation, it was also, as a metaphor for a page, ripe for culture. Thoreau's agricultural and cultural labors, which were "accompaniments" to one another, yielded crops "instant and immeasurable." His labors rooted him in the instantaneous and in nature and linked him to the ethereal. That Thoreau described writing in agricultural metaphors suggested that one could think no better than one worked and ate daily. Life was a whole, and *Walden* represented an attempt to purge it of impurities. But *Walden* and Walden Pond were not the final form of metamorphosis; they were only experiments in integrity, economy, sublimation. There were more forms to be tested, other materials to be done without. Walden, as a habitat and a skin, could be shed, too. Perhaps, as Thoreau remarked wryly, he would discover some day that he could subsist—and blossom—on "board nails" only.

Private Discourse in Thoreau's *Walden*

Ronald B. Shwartz

I have engaged over the years in something of a lover's quarrel with *Walden:* it often bores me when I'm near it, and enchants me all the rest of the time. This seems rather extraordinary, as though my infatuation—I use that word consciously, insistently—were not with *Walden* but with some "idea" of *Walden,* one step removed and recollected in tranquility. This paper may properly be regarded as a study of my boredom-love-boredom-love-boredom-love, of a stubborn residuum of appreciation. I certainly make no claim to being the first to recognize the boring quality of *Walden.* Nathaniel Hawthorne called Thoreau a bore; so did the critic Theodore Baird. Even Thoreau called himself a bore, though he wasn't referring to Thoreau the writer of *Walden.* Stanley Cavell admitted that "it cannot, I think, be denied that *Walden* sometimes seems an enormously long and boring book." I consider this response sound but disagree that it reflects, as Cavell has suggested, "a boredom not of emptiness but of prolonged urgency." That remark strikes me as pretentious, the sort of intrepid speculation that gives literary criticism both sustenance and popular disrepute. I submit that we should respect the capacity of *Walden* to bore us without being compelled to explain it away as something else.

If *Walden* is sometimes boring, it is precisely because Thoreau indulges in and aspires to convey an ethereal experience, an ethereal attitude toward the world, to which we are unaccustomed; he seeks to saturate us with this aura, this way-of-being-in-the-world. It's easy to miss this forest for the

From *The South Carolina Review* 13, no. 1 (Fall 1980). © 1980 by Clemson University.

trees in *Walden*. The profoundest, the most fragile, ineffable meaning that Thoreau can be said to have expressed in this book emerges elusively, almost by indirection. Its meaning—probably impossible to rearticulate—can best be thought of as an existential "flavor" or "texture" or "fragrance." Comprehending it requires a deliberate blurring of the focus, so to speak; we must *drift* with Thoreau. In this connection T. S. Eliot's statement that poetry "communicates" before it is "understood" seems instructive. Like poetry, *Walden* consists in a language of meaning which is highly personal yet not utterly opaque. The test for gauging the truth of this characterization is whether the unique discourse in *Walden* can be learned, used, and shared by would-be participants in the so-called "culture of argument" which Thoreau may be said to have created. Is it enough to observe, as critics so frequently have, that Thoreau employed history, anthropology, Scripture, paradox, irony, ridicule, philological puns, and [as Sherman Paul writes] "every variety of symbolic statement"; that he employed, to put it technically, oxymoron, alliteration, hyperbole, meiosis, synechdoche, metonomy, portmanteau words, anaphora, litotes, apostrophe, antistrophe, rhetorical questions, and climactic paragraph endings? What more does *Walden* do than simply "tell" us to simplify our affairs and to listen to our own drummer and to eschew material wealth and other superficialities and delusions, and to live what is truly life and to elevate by conscious endeavor the quality of our lives and to notice how wonderful nature is? Why are synopses of this sort grotesque and trite, and unfaithful to the text of *Walden*?

Like poetry, *Walden* moves delicately, often imperceptibly between the literal (that which we think we understand plainly) and the more conspicuously metaphorical, the allusive, the downright ambiguous. We are apt to feel confused, out of control, uncertain about what in *Walden* is metaphorical and what is less metaphorical, what if anything is completely secure from metaphor, what metaphors are more transparently tied to a single, discrete referent; and indeed whether it really matters that we always be sure. A good verb to describe what *Walden* does is "float" between the more literal and the less, between the material and the spiritual. Thoreau is taking us strenuously to the border of the language. "Give me that sentence," he wrote, "which no intelligence can understand." We are made vaguely aware that although his language is the source, it is not the simple and direct administrator of what is "expressed." Content and form coalesce as he seeks to work the English language overtime: "The volatile truth of our words should continually betray the inadequacy of the residual statement." If argument can proceed in this formidable discourse at all, the opposing advocates might very likely drop dead from exhaustion. For like poetry, *Walden* exhibits an extreme commitment to what language can be made to achieve. As the critic David Greene pointed out, "overwhelming evidence suggests that few writers have used words more consciously, and that few have been more aware of what exactly they were trying to do.

Ultimately, it seems to me, the language of meaning in *Walden* is designed not merely as a general prescription for life but as an aesthetic in the broadest sense, the aesthetic of putting a life in order, of being able to account for one's life, of making one's life clean and pure and simple and controlled in a way that reminds me of Hemingway (e.g., "A Clean, Well-Lighted Place," "The Big, Two-Hearted River") and Robert Frost. There is something very comforting, self-sufficient and charming in this appeal. Thoreau makes life subtly lyrical. One might say that *Walden* domesticates through resonant language the irritatingly obscure word "transcendental," makes it breathe. *Walden* does not merely "describe" or "illustrate" the *Walden* experience; in a real sense the language and the experience are inseparable; the feeling and the reflection upon it merge. In this regard Thoreau spoke of a certain "doubleness" in his experience: "I am conscious of the presence and criticism of a part of me, which, as it were, is not a part of me, but spectator, sharing no experience, but taking note of it." It may thus appear that the *Walden* experience was very much what the language of *Walden* is.

For purposes of analysis *Walden* might be divided roughly into two categories: (1) what the writer dislikes and seeks to reject; and (2) what the writer likes and seeks to promote. Probably the most characteristic way that Thoreau engages in the predominantly "negative" discourse is by retaining the vocabulary associated with that which he rejects and modulating it through obvious, mildly playful irony for his own purposes. Putting it more graphically, what Thoreau does is deflect the language of his opposition after a fashion analogous to the practitioner of jujitsu, who uses the strength and weight of his adversary to disable him. Thus, to consider the most prominent example, Thoreau inverts the traditional language of private property ownership (in "Where I Lived") by insisting that farms can be "bought" in our minds alone, that a man who can appreciate a farm without literally buying it can, like Thoreau, be "a rich man without any damage to my poverty"; that a man is "rich" in proportion to the number of things he can "afford" to let alone. This deliberate muddling of language serves, in effect, to remove the ground from under our feet, to induce the kind of exquisite, even amusing, disorder that Socrates typically induced in his disciples: "Now, to speak the truth, I had but ten cents in the world, and it surpassed my arithmetic to tell, if I was the man who had ten cents, or who had the farm, or ten dollars, or all together." But whereas Socrates asks: "Is this what we really mean, or should mean, by so and so?" Thoreau asks the same question in a less vigorously logical, more poetic way. Both men subvert the common understanding briskly, yet both can be viewed as neglecting to furnish a specific, tangible alternative. In *Walden,* this form of discourse can thus seem evasive, bothersome, oxymoronic for its own sake. "I never found the companion that was so companionable as solitude," Thoreau writes. And again: "silence alone is worthy to be heard"; and "not till we are lost . . . do we begin to find ourselves"; and "I have always been regretting that I was not as wise as the day I was born." As a discrete form of discourse, such language may seem facile; it is apparently what prompted one critic to explain that Thoreau "speaks as an exception to every rule, the judge of all the rest of the universe, droning on and on, monotonously didactic, deliberately obscure. Argument proceeding in this discourse of ironic inversions would almost necessarily be stillborn, for Thoreau is always willing to respond to an assertion by incorporating its vocabulary into his own personal schema. Thoreau, in part, is a verbal amoeba.

The risk of unintelligibility here is great. There is the passage in "Solitude," for example, where Thoreau rejects the conventional meaning of such words as "loneliness," "space," and "distance," and highlights the difference between the mundane way and his own way of having and talking about experience:

> Men frequently say to me, "I should think you would feel lonesome down there, and want to be nearer to folks, rainy and snowy days and nights especially." I am tempted to reply to such,—This whole earth which we inhabit is but a point in space. How far apart, think you, dwell the two most distant inhabitants of yonder star . . . Why should I feel lonely? is not our planet in the Milky Way . . . What sort of space is that which separates a man from his fellows and makes him solitary? . . . What do we want most to dwell near to? Not to many men, surely . . . but to the perennial source of our life."

Thoreau is not mad; rather, he is doing his best with a language which is not ordinarily employed to accommodate his experience in this world, his *Weltansicht.* It is therefore no wonder that his language seems alien or cryptic, attuned to a different frequency; that he does not feel at home with pedestrian utterances about the world. Inasmuch as Thoreau's "negative" discourse (1) merely rejects conventional words registering conventional experience, and (2) merely replaces such words, if at all, with conclusory labels for his own idiosyncratic experience (e.g., "the universe constantly and obediently answers to our conceptions," "explore your own higher latitudes," "in eternity there is indeed something true and sublime," "we crave only reality"), his discourse remains essentially a black box to the rest of the world; had he replied to the townsmen who thought he was lonely they would not have understood. They reside in a separate sphere.

When Thoreau writes in the so-called "positive" mode, his prose can be said to "enact," rather than merely express "directly," his meaning. The reason for this, of course, is that Thoreau's meaning is, seemingly at least, too subtle to be conveyed by language-as-mere-conduit; hence the form of the language must conspire artfully with whatever meaning his words would otherwise bear, and the result is nothing less than a prose-poem, of which *Walden* exhibits several varieties. First, in what is perhaps the quintessential passage of the book, Thoreau writes:

> I went to the woods because I wished to live deliberately, to front only the essential facts of life, and see if I could not learn what it had to teach, and not, when I came to die, discover that I had not lived. I did not wish to live what was not life, living is so dear; nor did I wish to practise resignation, unless it was quite necessary. I wanted to live deep and suck out all the marrow of life, to live so sturdily and Spartan-like as to put to rout all that was not life, to cut a broad swath and shave close, to drive life into a corner, and reduce it to its lowest terms, and, if it proved mean, why then to get the whole and genuine meanness of it, and publish its meanness to the world; or if it were sublime, to know it by experience, and be able to give a true account of it in my next excursion.

Like much of Thoreau's prose the passage, if taken on its face, conveys a mere penumbra of its more penetrating meaning and could just as adequately have been expressed as: "I wanted to find out what life was about, and then live it up!" Yet if yielded to, gazed at impressionistically, the passage communicates (or if you like, "argues" for) that which resists paraphrase. The language, it may be said, radiates with a meaning that derives, not from any one particular "device," but from the confluence of its many features. These features include the cadence of the sentences, retarded by an abundance of monosyllabic words and accentuated by the repetition of "I," and the repetition of infinitive clauses (and the clause "to live," in particular). The function of simplicities in this discourse is pronounced; just as Thoreau seeks to reduce life to "its lowest terms" (whatever that may mean), he reduces language to *its* lowest terms, demanding the strictest economy of style (note the spareness of the words "went," "wished," "live," "life," "see," "learn," "came," "die," "facts," and the simple elegance of the clause "living is so dear," which is suspended breathlessly, demurely, after the longer clause which it modifies). The mélange of hyperactive metaphors in the latter half of the passage contrasts with the scarcity of metaphors in the former half, thus suggesting, without articulating, a meditation on the world which is at once simple yet vibrant. This singular passion for "reality" is unsusceptible to refutation, and therein lies the paradox: argument in this discourse is foreclosed because to participate in its language is perforce to concede the meaning that such language uniquely conceives. This is to say that in a language where "style of argument" and "the argument itself" are so intimate, so equivocally fused, as they are in *Walden,* argument cannot proceed within that language, because any two persons who can be said to share such language—assuming that they could—would quite literally have nothing to argue about. To invoke a legal metaphor, the language is the natural monopoly of its meaning.

Another and especially typical way that Thoreau generates a personal language of meaning through the performance of language is by proliferating a rich "accounting" of observations. This is the aesthetic of immersing one's soul, if you will, in the hot bath of crisp, solid, delicious facts, and the bath of words articulating these facts. That we are compelled to resort to metaphor in describing what Thoreau does is telling; we apprehend that what is most central to his language of meaning is itself wordless, hovering somehow above the language itself. It seems insufficient to say that what Thoreau values here is an aesthetic of exactness, an affection for something "solid," something that a person can grab on to; that taking inventory on observable facts can be the pastime of a sublime maturity: "Walden," he wrote,

> is blue at one time and green at another, even from the same point of view. Lying between the earth and the heavens, it partakes of the color of both. Viewed from a hill-top it reflects the color of the sky; but near at hand it is of a yellowish tint next the shore where you can see the sand, then a light green, which gradually deepens to a uniform dark green in the body of the pond. In some lights, viewed even from a hill-top it is of a vivid green next the shore. Some have referred this to the reflection of the verdure; but it is equally green there against the railroad

sand-bank, and in the spring, before the leaves are expanded, and it may be simply the result of the prevailing blue mixed with the yellow of the sand.

("The Ponds")

These are the musings of a quivering, probing, staid sensibility; this is how Thoreau tastes the world. And in taste, as it were, there is no dispute.

A third way that Thoreau seeks to capture the preciousness of his experience is through what might be called "loud" metaphors, symbols, and parables. Like all of his positive discourse, this mode demonstrates, in all its variations, that Thoreau, standing on the geographical and existential periphery of society, must correspondingly discover and make use of the periphery of the English language; that insofar as new ways of experiencing the world are not amenable to rational or scientific confirmation, they are definable only in terms of language which is unfamiliar and relatively private. This language aborts arguments, for it represents a special claim— not merely that "my way of experiencing the world is a true one," but that it is a private and unexpressible yet somewhat sharable one. Implicit here is the claim, always available in case the writer is controverted, that "it isn't that you disagree but rather that you don't understand." That claim is of course available in most argument but its potency in this discourse is particularly significant. Thoreau's discourse is such that his meaning cannot readily be impugned because it cannot be pinned down. He tells us, for example, that

as I drew a still fresher soil about the rows with my hoe, I disturbed the ashes of unchronicled nations who in primeval years lived under these heavens, and their small implements of war and hunting were brought to the light of this modern day. They lay mingled with other natural stones, some of which bore the marks of having been burned by Indian fires, and some by the sun, and also bits of pottery and glass brought hither by the recent cultivators of the soil. When my hoe tinkled against the stones, that music echoed to the woods and the sky, and was an accompaniment to my labor which yielded an instant and immeasurable crop. It was no longer beans that I hoed, nor I that hoed beans.

Understanding what this passage means in any absolute sense is probably impossible. The metaphor must be acquiesced in, not clearly apprehended. Its ambiguity, its elusiveness, must be accepted; for Thoreau seeks to communicate what may be called intellectually rarefied feelings. When such feelings are the very stuff of a discourse, as they are in *Walden,* then would-be counterargument in that same discourse crumbles in our hands. Thoreau's discourse is thus his fortress as well; it insulates him.

In a Platonic dialogue like the *Gorgias,* in contrast to *Walden,* discourse proceeds with extreme syllogistic precision. First, the advocate (Socrates) establishes a common ground, some assertion which is manifestly true, at least to the participants. He then proceeds to show that this initial assertion necessarily implies (1) another but more controversial assertion posited by the advocate, and/or (2) the opposite of some assertion posited by the opposing advocate. The only analogue to this discourse in *Walden* consists in movement from the "common ground" of literal fact and then proceeding to introduce the more figurative. Most of the chapters in *Walden,* it is true, begin concretely; their first sentences are readily comprehensible. (See, e.g., "Economy," "Where I Lived," "The Bean-Field," "The Village," "The Ponds," "Brute Neighbors," "House-Warming," "Former Inhabitants," "Winter Animals," and "Spring.") The "turn" in the argument, however, goes unchecked in *Walden;* it lacks the distinct incremental steps and strictly logical connections of the *Gorgias* and depends instead on what may be called, for lack of a better term, the imaginative leap. Whereas the *Gorgias* discourse proceeds almost like a finely tuned machine, the *Walden* discourse proceeds like a ballet. In both discourses the broad appeal is to truth, but whereas in the *Gorgias* this appeal is primarily to logic, the appeal in *Walden* is to something else, to a certain sympathy. The difference is fundamental. In the *Gorgias,* argument can proceed methodically: when apparent contradictions arise either the contradiction is reconciled or the self-contradictory party concedes. But in *Walden,* the only real authority, essentially, is the discourser himself, who easily becomes, for purposes of the argument at hand, omniscient. Inadvertently or not, *Walden* might be said to entail the same claim to inexorability as art or music. Both involve the same unilateral porousness, which is to say that meaning filters outward but refutation is futile, itself absurd.

In *Walden,* furthermore, private experience is not only the resource but the salient limitation of Thoreau's discourse. *Walden* might well be considered a *fictional* discourse, which is to say that it is an insufficient language for talking about the world and improving it, and that it cannot be regarded as altogether "successful" even when judged by its own stated purposes. Thoreau claims to address "mainly the mass of men who are discontented, and idly complaining of the hardness of their lot or of the times, when they might improve them." But does *Walden,* qua recommendation for living, play ostrich, so to speak; does it fail to negotiate with the so-called Real World? Granted that Thoreau does not recommend that the masses abandon their affairs and take up residence in proximity to a pond. But if not that, what? Can the simplification of life or the living of "life near the bone" really improve the quality of life? Is this a realistic pursuit for all those who lack Thoreau's mental and emotional faculties and who cannot find poignancy in the mundane? Does it necessarily follow that because we can participate in and feel that we "appreciate," more or less, the experience that the *Walden* discourse exudes, we can enjoy a comparable experience on our own, that we can emancipate ourselves into a world of incessant novelty and freshness and vivaciousness, or anything close to it? Is it enough to say, as Thoreau does, that "a man . . . must maintain himself in whatever attitude he finds himself through obedience to the laws of his being which will never be one of opposition to a just government"? Are there no psychological or socioeconomic constraints on the ability of modern men to assimilate *Walden* into their lives? These questions obviously import the imponderables, but they are certainly not answered in a book which shows only that one man, Thoreau, could enjoy the kind of experience that *Walden* represents and espouses. *Walden* is plausible as a language of meaning, but as an argument for what all men can do for themselves, for their consciousnesses, it is not; as such its persuasiveness rests on our faith in the sacred text that *Walden* may inspire us to believe it is.

Houses and Compost: Thoreau's *Walden*

Joseph G. Kronick

In *Nature,* Emerson told his readers, " 'Build therefore your own world' ";
Thoreau went to Walden Pond to build a house and write a book. The two
tasks, building and writing, were one and the same for Thoreau. Like
Whitman, he could never be content as "any man's mere follower"; he
would build his own house, even if it was on Emerson's property.

A journal entry for January 1, 1852, reveals the close association books
and homes had for Thoreau: "I wish to survey my composition for a
moment from the least favorable point of view. I wish to be translated to
the future, and look at my work as it were at a structure on the plain, to
observe what portions have crumbled under the influence of the elements."
Thoreau desires not only to be "translated to the future" but also to translate
the book into a house and thereby leave a sturdy edifice. But he knows
that some of it will erode with time, leaving only archives, fragments of a
foundation. The building of a house is not unlike the writing of a book;
they both require a firm foundation and solid financing: "When I consider
how our homes are built and paid for, or not paid for, and their internal
economy managed and sustained, I wonder that the floor does not give
way under the visitor while he is admiring the gewgaws upon the mantle-
piece, and let him through into the cellar, to some solid and honest though
earthy foundation." The search for an earthy foundation is a search for a
point d'appui, "a place," writes Walter Michaels [in "*Walden's* False Bottoms"], "we locate by asking questions. We know that we've found it when

From *American Poetics of History: From Emerson to the Moderns.* © 1984 by Louisiana
State University Press.

one of our questions is answered. The name we give to this place is Nature. The search for solid bottom is a search for . . . what is real, that is, natural, and not human." Thoreau's objection to houses can be read as an objection to all human institutions, including language. Nietzsche called language a prison house; Thoreau thought all houses were prisons. Yet Thoreau does build his house; he even "took particular pleasure in this breaking of ground [digging the cellar]. . . . Under the most splendid house in the city is still to be found the cellar where they store their roots as of old, and long after the superstructure has disappeared posterity remark its dent in the earth."

In his eulogy for Thoreau, Emerson says Thoreau preferred New England to Europe because New England "is not based on any Roman ruins. We have not to lay the foundation of our houses on the ashes of a former civilization." Thoreau will be his own architect, or technician of the *archē* (that is the maker of origins), and lay the ruins for future generations. It is the foreign architect who arouses Thoreau's anger. The breaking of the ground is the inscription of an origin. Thoreau turns the fields and woods surrounding Walden Pond into a text. His sentences dig furrows in the ground marking the presence of the dweller. In a fascinating passage on Rousseau, Derrida comments on the *via rupta,* plowing and writing: "The furrow of agriculture, we remind ourselves, opens nature to culture (cultivation). And one also knows that writing is born with agriculture which happens only with sedentarization." Writing by furrows means that the linear movement remains unbroken as the line transverses from left to right and then right to left. Opening nature to culture involves a reordering of space that reveals the presence of man. In terms of writing, the space of the sentence marks the presence of the author; in other words, writing is consciousness becoming spatial. The objective of reading would be to erase the signifier (i.e., writing) and recover the signified (i.e., the author's consciousness). But this recovery of presence can only be thought of within writing, a system of representation owing as much to reading as it does to inscription. Writing does not follow the line of the plowman; reading by furrows is easier than writing by furrows. Writing is determined as much by the hand as by the eye. As Derrida puts it [in *Of Grammatology*], "One does not only write, one reads a little blindly, guided by the order of the hand." The successive movement of the written line breaks up the linear progression of agriculture. Writing doesn't exist in a genetic line running from consciousness to the sensible world. As writing is only intelligible by virtue of repetition—by occupying the space of reading—it represents a consciousness locked in a chain of signifiers.

In *Walden,* Thoreau refuses to acknowledge the doubleness of writing. Writing is always a reading and, therefore, can never be original. He would like to think of the writer as a maker, a man of action. The writer, for Thoreau, occupies that place which brings together nature and culture. But the writer, who should thus be a bringer of harmony, brings violence instead. The excess of writing transgresses the silent harmony of nature: "The volatile truth of our words should continually betray the inadequacy of the residual statement. Their truth is instantly *translated;* its literal monument alone remains." The ideal would be the erasure of the signifier, but ideals are hard to live up to. Let us turn to Thoreau on building, where we find only empty monuments, never truth.

Whenever Thoreau talks about building, he adopts the language of presence: "Architectural beauty . . . has gradually grown from within outward, out of the necessities and character of the indweller, who is the only builder." The language of this passage is remarkably Heideggerian. In "Building Dwelling Thinking," Heidegger writes, "*Only if we are capable of dwelling, only then can we build.*" And like Heidegger, Thoreau also believes that the proper sense of dwelling has been surpressed by the excrescences of civilization—that is, by ornament and language. For Thoreau, architectural ornaments copied from European models mark the absence of spirit: "It [building without dwelling] is of a piece with constructing his own coffin,—the architecture of the grave, and 'carpenter,' is but another name for 'coffin-maker.' " If we allow a foreign technician to construct our *archē,* we risk falling through the superstructure and landing upon the relics of decayed civilizations. Instead, we must find unbroken ground upon which to build our home.

A *point d'appui* therefore requires a deliberate dwelling in nature—an incision that marks the origin of an American culture. To allow another architect to construct the house is to exchange the home for a coffin. The importation of European architecture has its parallel in the problem of translation. According to Thoreau, it is not enough to read the classics "in the character of our mother tongue"; these works "will always be in a language dead to degenerate times." But even knowledge of the original language may not suffice. "Books must be read as deliberately and reservedly as they were written. It is not enough even to be able to speak the language of that nation by which they are written, for there is a memorable interval between the spoken and the written language, the language heard and the language read." The interval between speech and writing measures the progress from savagery to culture. It is the difference between dwelling outdoors or in a house of one's own; it is the advent of agriculture.

And as literature may be corrupted by the transcription from one country to another, so may architecture.

Let us pause to contrast Thoreau's rejection of translation with Emerson's praise for it. In a journal entry eventually used in "Books," Emerson writes:

> I thank the translators & it is never my practice to read any Latin, Greek, German, Italian, scarcely any French book, in the original which I can procure in an English translation. I like to be beholding to the great metropolitan English speech, the sea which receives tributaries from every region under heaven, the Rome of nations, and I should think it in me as much folly to read all my books in originals when I have them rendered for me in my mother's speech by men who have given years to the labor, as I should to swim across Charles River when ever I wished to go to Charlestown.

Their contrasting attitudes toward translation may explain their equally different attitudes toward originality. If there is no original text as Emerson says, then to read a book in English is merely to choose one translation over another. English would even be preferable—its fragmented and indeterminable origin makes it a universal language. Containing elements from all other nations, English is a bastard language: although the mother may be identifiable, there are many candidates for the father. Thoreau, a believer in origins, makes much more of reading in the original language, as he values the father more than the mother.

As we might expect, the genealogical implications of the metaphor of a mother tongue are not lost upon Thoreau. He says speech is "a sound, a tongue, a dialect merely, almost brutish, and we learn it unconsciously, like the brutes, of our mothers." Writing, however, "is the maturity and experience of that [speech]; if that is our mother tongue, this is our father tongue, a reserved and select expression, too significant to be heard by the ear, which we must be born again in order to speak." The emergence of writing signifies a spiritual growth in society, as Thoreau's allusion to John 3:3 indicates. But writing has other associations. Derrida points out that "the birth of writing (in the colloquial sense) was nearly everywhere and most often linked to genealogical anxiety." Those roots in Thoreau's cellar aren't just potatoes; they are the ancestors' (metaphorical?) remains. The incision of the line doesn't break new ground; instead, it reveals the path that has already been dug.

We need not be surprised that, however much Thoreau may insist on writing as the spiritual father, he favors speech. When he says writing "is the work of art nearest to life itself," he resorts to metaphors of self and presence: "It [the written word] may be translated into every language, and not only be read but actually breathed from all human lips;—not be represented on canvas or in marble only, but be carved out of the breath of life itself. *The symbol of an ancient man's thought becomes a modern man's speech*" (my emphasis).

The written word is the transcription of a thought that awaits resurrection by the reader; in this, Thoreau's theory of reading resembles Emerson's. Thoreau, however, adheres more closely than does Emerson to the traditional metaphysics of presence—speech is the sign of presence, and writing is the substitute for speech. Writing represents, not presence, but the signs of presence. Speech guarantees the life of mind and culture. Thoreau also shares Emerson's belief that nature is a book: "The earth expresses itself outwardly in leaves, it so labors with the idea inwardly." (It's worth noting that this inside/outside metaphor operates within the same conceptual system as do thought/speech and writing/reading.) The pun on *leaf* appears again when he asks, "What Champollion will decipher this hieroglyphic for us, that we may turn over a new leaf at last?"

The work of deciphering leads us back to the earth. Thoreau writes in a journal entry for October 16, 1859: "Talk about learning our *letters* and being *literate!* Why, the roots of *letters* are *things.* Natural objects and phenomena are the original symbols or types which express our thoughts and feelings, and yet American scholars, having little or no root in the soil, commonly strive with all their might to confine themselves to the imported symbols alone. All the true growth and experience, the living speech, they would fain reject as 'Americanisms.' . . . A more intimate knowledge, a deeper experience, will surely originate a word." Just as our architecture and literature are borrowed, so is our very vocabulary. But Thoreau's alternative to foreign borrowings is a local borrowing. As the newly dug cellar uncovered the roots of the ancestors, so will the roots of words prove to lie in more words, not in things. The "deeper experience" sought by Thoreau leads to a search for a *point d'appui,* which is a search for nature. By digging through the excrescences of civilization, he hopes to uncover nature and, consequently, "the living speech." Writing would thereby fall among the rubble of civilization as Thoreau seeks to break the chains placed upon him by conventions and foreign sources. There must be *extra vagance,* an opening of boundaries for the presence of the poet to emerge on the horizon. Thoreau writes, "I fear chiefly lest my expression may not be *extra-vagant* enough, may not wander far enough beyond the narrow limits of my daily experience, so as to be adequate to the truth of which I have been convinced. *Extra vagance!* it depends on how you are yarded." (Thoreau's puns, like his living alone in the woods, are a movement outside the boundaries, the decorum, of New England society.)

His desire for extra vagance resembles the Heideggerian sense of boundary as that "from which something *begins its presencing.*" I would like to return once more to Heidegger's essay "Building Dwelling Thinking" for an analysis of the horizon. Heidegger says, "A boundary is not that at which something stops but, as the Greeks recognized, the boundary is that from which something *begins its presencing.* That is why the concept is that of *horismos,* that is, the horizon, the boundary. Space is the essence that for which room has been made, that which is let into its bounds." The digging of the cellar and the erecting of the house at Walden Pond form the site where Thoreau begins his presencing. Thoreau's yard does not pen him in; rather, it allows for the location, as Heidegger explains it, "into which earth and heaven, divinities and mortals are admitted." But if the horizon is the site where presencing begins, it is also the site where presence remains almost, but never quite, present. Thoreau aims to recover full presence, the living speech; the poet's task, however, is one of inscription—digging and writing. Thoreau's wandering beyond boundaries leads him into the boundary's path. The effacement of boundaries that promises the emergence of the poet's presence comes to displace presence within the "structure of the trace." Yet this structure has no place; it is effaced by an inscription that "constitutes it as a trace."

Emerson calls the tracing of traces "quotation," and its emblem is the horizon. In "Experience" he writes, "Men seem to have learned of the horizon the art of perpetual retreating and reference. . . . I quote another man's saying; unluckily that other withdraws himself in the same way, and quotes me." As the sign of the approaching or retreating sun, the horizon serves as a sign for that which refers beyond itself to what it can never re-present. And, as we have seen, the writer, who is only a quoter, is never present. For, as Emerson suggests, to assert oneself is to withdraw one's self—the voice is the sign of the speaker's absence.

Thoreau, on the other hand, wishes to recover and assert presence. He speaks of presencing as taking place in both time and space. Time for transcendentalists, particularly Kantian ones, is recognized as a product of mind, and it can only be measured in terms of space. Thoreau employs metaphors of space when expressing his desire "to improve the nick of time, and notch it on my stick too; to stand on the meeting of two eternities, the past and the future, which is precisely the present moment; to toe that line." What is this stick but a stylus, a pen? Thoreau's dwelling clears a space for the boundary within which he begins his presencing—declares his independence by writing his first book, *A Week on the Concord and Merrimack Rivers*. His objection to speech is that it is common—he must learn it from others. But by writing, he gains the mastery of the pen, which we might call a phallus, and in rewriting history, he inscribes his own origin. The master of the pen/phallus becomes his own father.

We must turn to *Walden*'s conclusion and the fable of the artist of Kouroo to see how writing, genealogy, and history are linked in Thoreau's text. Like Thoreau, the artist of Kouroo also carves a stick, but rather than notch the nick of time on it, he uses it to write the end of time in the sand: "Before he had given it the proper shape the dynasty of the Condahars was at an end, and with the point of the stick he wrote the name of the last of the race in the sand, and then resumed his work." The fable of the writer and his stick is Thoreau's inscribing of the boundary from which he will begin his presencing. But the possessor of the stylus does not master time; he can only translate it into the relic of the book. Thoreau wishes to master time through art. His book will set him free from history; but as the concluding fable shows, writing inscribes, even commemorates, the passage of time. Time is only thinkable within the path of the line, which the artist's stick traces. In spite of what his text tells him, Thoreau wishes to be the author—that is, the codifier of his own origin and the father of American literature. Ideally, the two origins would be connate. Let us turn to a journal entry for December 27, 1855, in which he lists the important dates in his life that a biographer would want to record: "Was graduated in 1837(?). Began the big Red Journal, October, 1837. Found first arrowheads, fall of 1837. Wrote a lecture (my first) on Society, March 14th, 1838, and read it before the Lyceum." Thoreau's careers as writer, lecturer, autobiographer, and archaeologist begin with the recognition of his belatedness. He, too, must build on the ruins of another culture, one that has better claims to the home than does his own. His topic, society, is further proof of the distance from the origin of culture.

Although Thoreau saw fit to devote a chapter to reading in *Walden*, it is sounds, after all, that guarantee spirit and originality. If we only read books, Thoreau writes, "we are in danger of forgetting the language which all things and events speak without metaphor, which alone is copious and standard." Echoing the sentiment of Emerson's question "Why should not we also enjoy an original relation to the universe?" Thoreau asks, "Will you be a reader, a student merely, or a seer?" Thoreau looks upon nature as accessible to him who lives deliberately. The reader, then, is secondary;

only the writer enjoys an original relation to the universe. But he can be original only by forgetting his belatedness; the writer must forget he is also a reader. Thoreau makes this clear when he says, "I did not read books the first summer; I hoed beans." In *Walden,* hoeing is synonymous with writing. He did not hoe beans so he could eat them, but "for the sake of tropes and expressions, to serve a parable-maker one day." But he breaks ground only to find remains of his precursors. Even he admits, "Decayed literature makes the richest of soils."

If Thoreau says culture is fertilizer, it's only because the world is a compost heap. The hieroglyphic of nature, Thoreau says, "is somewhat excrementitious in its character, and there is no end to the heaps of liver, lights, and bowels, as if the globe were turned wrong side outward; but this suggests at least that Nature has some bowels, and there again is mother of humanity." Growing out of this compost is language. Sitting by a railroad cut, Thoreau remarks: "You find thus in the very sands an anticipation of the vegetable leaf. . . . The overhanging leaf sees here its prototype. *Internally,* whether in the globe or animal body, it is a moist thick *lobe,* a word especially applicable to the liver and lungs and the *leaves* of fat, (λειβω, *labor, lapsus,* to flow or slip downward, a lapsing; λοβόſ, *globus,* lobe, globe; also lap, flap, and many other words), *externally,* a dry thin *leaf,* even as the *f* and *v* are a pressed and dried *b.*" In examining this passage and its debt to Walter Whiter's theory of a universal language, Michael West comments [in *Walden's* Dirty Language] that "life and language are not only coordinates, but all life seems to aspire to linguistic expression." To idealize this passage is to deny evidence of Thoreau's anxiety over his belatedness. Rather than give birth to living speech, the world will only permit the recomposition of a decomposed language. After all, *compost,* as the *OED* informs us, means both manure and literature.

Stanley Cavell takes a more humanistic view of Thoreau's metaphors. "In *Walden,*" he writes, "reading is not merely the other side of writing, its eventual fate; it is another metaphor for writing itself. The writer cannot invent words as 'perpetual suggestions and provocations'; the written word is already 'the choicest of relics.' " Although Cavell sees writing and reading as analogous activities, the writer bears "a commitment to total and transparent meaning" that the reader is obliged to recover. Cavell, like Thoreau, subordinates reading to writing. The writer escapes the secondariness of a reader by uncovering the sediment that has accumulated upon words and restoring their "transparent meaning." In effect, Cavell separates writing from reading. The recovery of lost time—that is, the assertion of originality—is to be accomplished by writing, which is spatial. But Thoreau's hoeing metaphors overturn Cavell's claim for a temporal recovery of presence. A deliberate dwelling, on the contrary, does not bring us into relation with nature. While hoeing, Thoreau does not recover the object; he uncovers "tropes and expressions"—metaphors—and metaphors are borrowed homes. Tropes are words which can be occupied by several meanings, none of which may dwell there permanently. And as agriculture affirms the presence of society and the loss of virgin nature, writing affirms that "meaning" is always already borrowed from the dung heap of literature upon which the foundation of *Walden* is built.

A final aside is in order here. We have heard from Melville and Emerson on the hopeless task of the geologist. It is only fitting that we allow Thoreau to contradict Emerson once more: "The earth is not a mere fragment of dead history, stratum upon stratum like the leaves of a book, to be studied by geologists and antiquaries chiefly, but living poetry like the leaves of a tree, which precede flowers and fruit,—not a fossil earth, but a living earth; compared with whose great central life all animal and vegetable life is merely parasitic. Its throes will heave our exuviae from their graves." But Thoreau has just finished telling us that the living earth, which now appears to be in its death throes, is a heap of excrement. He wants to revivify nature by turning excrement into life, just as he wants to turn his geological metaphor into an organic metaphor. Thoreau stands self-condemned, since the site of his hut by the side of Walden Pond was a short distance beyond Emerson's home. In a discussion of host and parasite, J. Hillis Miller comes to the following conclusions on the definitions and etymologies of the Greek prefix *para:*

> "Para" is an "uncanny" double antithetical prefix signifying at once proximity and distance, similarity and difference, interiority and exteriority, something at once inside a domestic economy and outside it, something simultaneously this side of the boundary line, threshold, or margin, and at the same time beyond it, equivalent in status and at the same time secondary or subsidiary, submissive, as of guest to host, slave to master. A thing in "para" is, moreover, not only simultaneously on both sides of the boundary line between inside and outside. It is also the boundary itself, the screen which is at once a permeable membrane connecting inside and outside, confusing them with one another, allowing the outside in, making the inside out, dividing them but also forming an ambiguous transition between one and the other.

Thoreau's desire for extra vagance depends upon a distinct boundary within which he will be master—a place where contact with the particularities of nature will give rise to universal truth. But Thoreau is both master and slave. He boasts of living within his slight domestic economy, but he fails to say that he lives within his domicile by leaving his domestic economy to Emerson's charity—the house, after all, was built on Emerson's property.

We need to mention one more of Emerson's tenants, Whitman, who, like Thoreau, rejects the nihilism of the geological metaphor and turns to an organic metaphor in its place: "The science of language has large and close analogies in geological science, with its ceaseless evolution, its fossils, and its numberless submerged layers and hidden strata, the infinite go-before of the present. Or, perhaps Language is more like some vast living body, or perennial body of bodies. And slang not only brings the first feeders of it, but is afterward the start of fancy, imagination and humor, breathing into its nostrils the breath of life." Apparently, both Whitman and Thoreau had in mind the following passage from Emerson's essay "The Poet" when they wrote of geology and language:

> The poets made all the words, and therefore language is the archives of history, and, if we must say it, a sort of tomb of the muses. For though the origin of most of our words is forgotten, each word was at first a stroke of genius, and obtained currency because for the moment it symbolized the world to the first speaker and to the hearer. The etymologist finds the deadest word to have been once a brilliant picture. Language is fossil poetry. As the limestone of the continent consists of infinite masses of the shells of animalcules, so language is made up of images or tropes, which now, in their secondary use, have long ceased to remind us of their poetic origin.

Thoreau and Whitman want to affirm the poet's calling as the namer of things. They reject the skepticism that creeps into the following remark of Emerson's: "But the poet names the thing because he sees it, *or comes one step nearer to it than any other*" (my emphasis).

In "The Nature of Language," Heidegger writes of Stefan George, but he could just as well have been writing about American poets: "The decisive experience is that which the poet has undergone with the word—and the word inasmuch as it alone can bestow a relation to a thing. Stated more explicitly, the poet has experienced that only the word makes a thing appear as the thing is, and thus lets it be present. The word avows itself to the poet as that which holds and sustains a thing in its being. . . . The poet experiences his poetic calling as a call to the word as the source, the bourn of Being." What Thoreau fears is that the thing has been lost among the decomposed matter of language and nature. Just as he builds his hut with boards from a run-down shanty, so he composes his book out of the rotting remains of culture and nature. An inveterate punster, Thoreau hopes to regenerate a lost origin by exploiting the resources of language, particularly etymology. Thus, digging into the ground to build a firm foundation involves a recovery of the origin. This recovery is an uncanny (*unheimlich*) experience, as Freud finds out when tracing the etymology of *heimlich*: "What is *heimlich* thus comes to be *unheimlich*." Thoreau experiences the uncanny as poetic naming—his puns obscure the thing as much as they sustain it. By punning, Thoreau attempts to restore the antithetical sense of words that have been worn down to a simple definition. But this un-covering of meaning is a fragmenting of origins—puns reveal the indeter-minacy of language. No wonder Thoreau complains that "in this part of the world it is considered a ground for complaint if a man's writings admit of more than one interpretation."

Thoreau set out to build a house, but ended up with a compost heap. The history of American literature proves to be less a beginning than a continual destruction of the old. Emerson, who was capable of speaking of America as the new Eden, knew that literature thrives more on violence than it does on humanity: "The new continents are built out of the ruins of an old planet; the new races fed out of the decomposition of the foregoing. New arts destroy the old." The American writer is always discovering that the road west leads east of Eden.

*W*alden and the "Curse of Trade"

Michael T. Gilmore

Among the many paradoxes of *Walden* perhaps none is more ironic than the fact that this modernist text—modernist in its celebration of private consciousness, its aestheticizing of experience, its demands upon the reader—starts out as a denunciation of modernity. It is inspired by the agrarian ideals of the past, yet in making a metaphor of those ideals it fails as a rejoinder to the nineteenth century and creates as many problems as it lays to rest. Personal and historical disappointment determines the shape of Thoreau's masterpiece. In important ways it is a defeated text. Though Thoreau begins with the conviction that literature can change the world, the aesthetic strategies he adopts to accomplish political objectives involve him in a series of withdrawals from history; in each case the ahistorical maneuver disables the political and is compromised by the very historical moment it seeks to repudiate.

This is not to deny *Walden*'s greatness, but rather to emphasize the cost of Thoreau's achievement and to begin to specify its limits. No reader of the book can fail to notice the exultant tone of the "Conclusion"; the impression it leaves is of an author who has made good on his promise not to write "an ode to dejection." But one might say, in another paradox, that *Walden*'s triumphant success is precisely what constitutes its defeat. For underlying that triumph is a forsaking of civic aspirations for an exclusive concern with "the art of living well" (in Emerson's phrase about his former disciple). And to say this is to suggest that *Walden* is a book at odds with

From *American Romanticism and the Marketplace.* © 1985 by the University of Chicago. University of Chicago Press, 1985.

its own beliefs; it is to point out Thoreau's complicity in the ideological universe he abhors.

II

At the heart of Thoreau's dissent from modernity is a profound hostility to the process of change, to what he calls the "curse of trade." He pictures a contemporary Concord where everyone is implicated in the market, and he mounts a critique of that society as antithetical to independence, to identity, and to life itself. His antimarket attitude, though it has similarities to pastoralism, is more properly understood as a nineteenth-century revision of the agrarian or civic humanist tradition. Civic humanists regarded the economic autonomy of the individual as the basis for his membership in the polis. The self-sufficient owner of the soil, in their view, was the ideal citizen because he relied on his own property and exertions for his livelihood and was virtually immune to compromising pressures. Commercial enterprise, in contrast, endangered liberty because it fostered dependence on others and, by legitimating the pursuit of private interest, undermined devotion to the common good. Jeffersonian agrarianism, the American development of this tradition, retained its antimarket bias and its stress on freedom from the wills of others. In Jefferson's own formulation from the *Notes on the State of Virginia,* commerce is productive of subservience, and the independent husbandman uniquely capable of civic virtue.

Thoreau, writing some sixty years after Jefferson, shows a similar antipathy to exchange but entertains no illusions about either the present-day husbandman or the benefits conferred by real property. Several pages into *Walden* appears his well-known indictment of the various forms of ingratiation and venality practiced by his neighbors in order to make money—an indictment that applies to the farmer as much as to the tradesman.

> It is very evident what mean and sneaking lives many of you live, . . . always promising to pay, promising to pay, to-morrow, and dying to-day, insolvent; seeking to curry favor to get custom, by how many modes, only not state-prison offences; lying, flattering, voting [cf. Thoreau's attack on democracy in "Civil Disobedience"], contracting yourselves into a nutshell of civility, or dilating into an atmosphere of thin and vaporous generosity, that you may persuade your neighbor to let you make his shoes, or his hat, or his coat, or import his groceries for him.

Thoreau's position in this passage is directly opposed to the laissez-faire ideology gaining in popularity among his contemporaries. He sees the marketplace not as a discipline in self-reliance, an arena where the man of enterprise can prove his worth, but rather as a site of humiliation where the seller has to court and conciliate potential buyers to gain their custom. The interactions of exchange, in his view, breed not independence but servility. Nor, insists Thoreau, does nineteenth-century agriculture offer an exemption from the abasements and dependencies of the exchange process. The land has become an investment like any other and the farmer a willing participant in the marketplace. The husbandmen of Concord, immortalized by Emerson for their stand "by the rude bridge that arched the flood," are now "serfs of the soil" who spend their lives "buying and selling" and have forgotten the meaning of self-reliance. Thoreau envisions them, in a celebrated image, "creeping down the road of life," each pushing before him "a barn seventy-five feet by forty . . . and one hundred acres of land, tillage, mowing, pasture, and wood-lot!"

For Thoreau, commercial agriculture has an impact on the physical world which is just as devastating as its effect on the farmer. In the chapter "The Ponds" he describes an agriculture entrepreneur named Flint for whom nature exists solely as commodity. Indeed, on Flint's farm the use value of natural objects has been consumed by their exchange value; their abstract character as potential money has completely obliterated their "sensuous" reality (to use a favorite adjective of Marx's in this connection) as fruits and vegetables. The result is an impoverishment of the thing, an alteration of its very nature. "I respect not his labors," Thoreau writes of Flint,

> his farm where every thing has its price; who would carry the landscape, who would carry his God, to market, if he could get any thing for him; . . . on whose farm nothing grows free, whose fields bear no crops, whose meadows no flowers, whose trees no fruits, but dollars; who loves not the beauty of his fruits, whose fruits are not ripe for him till they are turned to dollars.

A companion chapter, "The Pond in Winter," shows this destruction of nature actually coming to pass through the speculations of "a gentleman farmer" who carries the landscape off to market. Wanting "to cover each one of his dollars with another," the farmer has hired a crew of laborers to strip Walden of its ice. Thoreau treats the entire operation as though the ice-cutters were "busy husbandmen" engaged in skimming the land: "They went to work at once, ploughing, harrowing, rolling, furrowing . . . [and]

suddenly began to hook up the virgin mould itself, with a peculiar jerk, clear down to the sand, or rather the water, . . . all the *terra firma* there was, and haul it away on sleds."

As Thoreau's denunciation of Flint makes clear, his quarrel with the marketplace is in large measure ontological. He sees the exchange process as emptying the world of its concrete reality and not only converting objects into dollars but causing their "it-ness" or being to disappear. A particularly powerful statement of this idea occurs at the beginning of "The Ponds," in the passage where Thoreau assails the marketing of huckleberries. He argues that nature's fruits "do not yield their true flavor" either to the man who raises them commercially or to their urban purchasers. The huckleberry cannot be tasted or even said to exist outside its native habitat: invariably it undergoes a fatal transformation en route from the countryside to the metropolis. What reaches Boston is not the fragrant berry itself but the "mere provender" that the fruit has become in being transported to the customer. Its bloom has been "rubbed off in the market cart" and its "ambrosial and essential part" extinguished by its conversion into an article of trade.

Thoreau believes that along with the degradation of the physical object in exchange there occurs a shriveling of the individual. Men in the marketplace, according to *Walden,* do not relate as persons but as something less than human; they commit violence against their own natures in their incessant anxiety to induce others to buy their products or their labor. "The finest qualities of our nature," Thoreau says in a passage paralleling his discussion of the huckleberry, "like the bloom on fruits, can be preserved only by the most delicate handling. Yet we do not treat ourselves or one another thus tenderly." The laborer's self, his authentic being, has as little chance to survive the exchange process as a genuine huckleberry. To satisfy his employer, he has to suppress his individuality and become a mechanical thing: "Actually, the laboring man has not leisure for a true integrity day by day; he cannot afford to sustain the manliest relations to men; his labor would be depreciated in the market. He has no time to be anything but a machine." The final disappearance of the person, the most extreme form of absence, would be death, and Thoreau does in fact equate exchange with the deprivation of life. "The cost of a thing," he writes, "is the amount of what I will call life which is required to be exchanged for it, immediately or in the long run." Exchange brings about the ultimate alienation of man from himself; to engage in buying and selling is not merely to debase the self but to extinguish it, to hurry into death.

Thoreau's analysis of commodification has certain affinities with the

Marxist critique of capitalism. His comments on the erosion of human presence in exchange evoke the notion of reification, a concept developed in the twentieth century by Georg Lukács. Reification refers to the phenomenon whereby a social relation between men assumes the character of a relation between things. Because they interact through the commodities they exchange, including the commodity of labor, individuals in the capitalist market confront each other not as human beings, but as objectified, nonhuman entities. They lose sight altogether of the subjective element in their activity. An important corollary to this loss of the person is a confusion of history with nature. By mystifying or obscuring man's involvement in the production of his social reality, reification leads him to apprehend that reality as a "second nature." He perceives the social realm as an immutable and universal order over which he exerts no control. The result is greatly to diminish the possibility of human freedom.

Thoreau reaches a similar conclusion about the decline of liberty under capitalism: he portrays his townsmen as slave-drivers of themselves. The weakness of his position, a weakness to which we shall return, is that he launches his attack against history rather than in its name, with the result that he mystifies the temporality of his own experience, presenting it as natural or removed from social time. He is outspoken in debunking such "naturalization" when it functions as a way of legitimating social codes. In his disquisition on clothing, for example, he points out how the fetishism of fashion invests the merely whimsical with the prestige of inevitability. "When I ask for a garment of a particular form," he explains, "my tailoress tells me gravely, 'They do not make them so now,' not emphasizing the 'They' at all, as if she quoted an authority as impersonal as the Fates. . . . We worship not the Graces, nor the Parcae, but Fashion."

Thoreau constantly challenges the false identification of what "they" say or do with the course of nature. He maintains that social reality, to which men submit as though to "a seeming fate," is in fact made by men and subject to their revision. His neighbors, whose resignation only masks their desperation, do not adopt the customary modes of living out of preference but "honestly think there is no choice left." Although they deny the possibility of change and say, "This is the only way," Thoreau insists that they are mistaken, that "there are as many ways" to live as "can be drawn radii from one centre." His lack of deference toward his elders stems from the same impatience with a reified social reality. Old people, he finds, regard their own experience as exemplary and refuse even to contemplate alternatives to the existing order of things. But "what old people say you cannot do you try and find that you can." What they fail to realize, what Thoreau feels all his neighbors are unable to see, is that "their daily life of routine and habit . . . is built on purely illusory foundations." They "think that *is* which *appears* to be."

III

To negate the "curse of trade" during his stay in the woods, Thoreau supports himself by farming. This is the occupation followed by the majority of his neighbors, but his own experiment in husbandry differs significantly from the commercial agriculture prevalent in Concord. By building his own house and growing his own food, by concentrating on the necessaries of life and renouncing luxuries, he minimizes his dependency on others and removes himself as far as possible from the market economy. In keeping with his precept, "Enjoy the land, but own it not," he squats on soil belonging to someone else (Emerson, as it happens) and endeavors to "avoid all trade and barter." "More independent than any farmer in Corcord," he claims to have learned from his experience that something approaching self-sufficiency is still practicable in mid-nineteenth-century America, if only "one would live simply and eat only the crop which he raised, and raise no more than he ate, and not exchange it for an insufficient quantity of more luxurious and expensive things."

Something *approaching* self-sufficiency: Thoreau makes no attempt to disguise the fact that he is unable to emancipate himself completely from exchange relations. He freely "publishes his guilt," as he puts it, that his venture at subsistence farming is not strictly speaking an economic success. He raises a cash crop of beans and uses the proceeds to give variety to his diet, and he is forced to supplement his income from farming by hiring himself out as a day laborer, the employment he finds "the most independent of any, especially as it required only thirty to forty days in a year to support one." He recognizes, in other words, the obsolescence of his program as a *literal* antidote to the ills of market civilization.

What Thoreau does affirm, and affirm consistently, is the possibility even in the nineteenth century of a way of life characterized by self-reliance and minimal involvement in exchange. Following the civic humanist tradition, he identifies this ideal with husbandry, and husbandry in turn supplies him with a metaphoric solution to the problems of the marketplace. Agriculture, he states, "was once a sacred art; but it is pursued with irreverent haste and heedlessness by us, our object being to have large farms and large crops merely." Thoreau makes a point of actually farming in the traditional way, going down to the woods and living by himself, because he refuses to sacrifice the use value of husbandry to its symbolic value in the manner of Flint. He wants to earn his metaphor by dwelling "near enough to Nature and Truth to borrow a trope from them."

Thoreau has an acute sense of the relationship between commodity and symbolism—or rather of the commodified thinking concealed in symbolization. The commodity, like the symbol, is both what it is and the token of something else (i.e., money); on Flint's farm, the something else has totally displaced the concrete reality. To use farming as a trope for self-sufficiency without literally farming would be to perform in thought the same violation Flint commits on his land. Thoreau finds this commodified habit of mind to be the common practice of his contemporaries. "Our lives," he complains, "pass at such remoteness from its symbols, and its metaphors and tropes are so far fetched." At Walden he redeems his own life from such distancing and loss of the real; he farms the land, as he says in "The Bean-Field," "for the sake of tropes and expression, to serve a parable-maker one day."

Thoreau suggest that the values formerly associated with farming are available to all men, in all pursuits. "Labor of the hands," as he describes his hoeing, "has a constant and imperishable moral, and to the scholar it yields a classic result." The moral yielded by *Walden* is that virtually any kind of workman can be a figurative farmer and any kind of work independent "labor of the hands." The centrality of this phrase to Thoreau's undertaking is suggested by its position at the very outset of the book; it appears in the opening sentence: "When I wrote the following pages, or rather the bulk of them, I lived alone, in the woods, a mile from any neighbor, in a house which I had built myself, on the shore of Walden Pond, in Concord, Massachusetts, and earned my living by the labor of my hands only." Labor of the hands is clearly meant to encompass intellectual as well as manual work. As Thoreau says in explaining what he lived for, "My head is hands and feet. I feel all my best faculties concentrated in it."

A difficulty that arises immediately with Thoreau's metaphoric solution to exchange is that it has the effect of privatizing a civic virtue. Farming as a way of life enjoyed the high standing it did in civic humanist thought because it was a training for participation in the public or political sphere. In *Walden,* as a figure for self-reliant labor, it has become a private virtue— a virtue without civic consequences. And there is no doubt that Thoreau hopes his text would result in some form of political awakening. Indeed, one of his principal objectives in writing *Walden* is to restore his countrymen to the freedom which they have lost under the market system. He moves to the woods on "Independence Day, or the fourth of July, 1845" because he considers this a civic enterprise, requiring a reformation or new foundation of American liberty. A close connection can be seen here between the project of *Walden* and Thoreau's appeal at the end of "Civil Disobedience" for a founder or reformer whose eloquence will revive the polity. In the essay, which he wrote while working on the early drafts of the book, he criticizes the country's lawmakers for their failure to "speak with authority" about the government. Implicitly he projects a role for himself as a model legislator, one whose effectiveness will lie in his ability to inspire others through his words:

> No man with a genius for legislation has appeared in America. They are rare in the history of the world. There are orators, politicians, and eloquent men, by the thousand; but the speaker has not yet opened his mouth to speak, who is capable of settling the much-vexed questions of the day. We love eloquence for its own sake; and not for any truth which it may utter, or any heroism it may inspire.

In *Walden* Thoreau assumes the duties of this reformer-legislator as a writer rather than a speaker because of the greater range and authority of literature. The orator, he says in the chapter "Reading," addresses the mob on the transitory issues of the moment, but the author "speaks to the heart and intellect of mankind, to all in any age who can *understand* him." Great writers, he adds, "are a natural and irresistible aristocracy in every society, and, more than kings or emperors, exert an influence on mankind." Twentieth-century readers, with their very different ideas about the functions of texts and the role of the writer, may find it difficult to take these statements seriously. But it is a mistake to treat *Walden* as though it were imbued with the modernist sentiment (to paraphrase W. H. Auden) that literature makes nothing happen. This kind of accommodation with "reality"—of reified consciousness—is precisely what Thoreau is arguing against in the book. Nor for the time and place is there anything especially unusual about his civic ambitions; on the contrary, they are perfectly consistent with the New England ideal of the literary vocation.

Lewis P. Simpson has shown that a conception of the writer as a spiritual and intellectual authority was particularly strong around Boston and Concord during the early decades of the nineteenth century. Simpson uses the term "clerisy," a borrowing from Coleridge, to designate the literary community that emerged at this time and sought to claim for men of letters the influence formerly exercised by the ministry. The wise and learned, it was felt, had a special obligation to educate the nation; through the practice of literature, they were to provide moral guidance and enlightenment. While Thoreau was hardly a conventional member of the New England elite, he shared his culture's emphasis on the usefulness of the literary calling. He conceives *Walden* as a reforming text meant to produce results in the world, and hopes to be remembered, like the heroic writers whom he so admires, as a "messenger" from heaven, [a] bearer of divine gifts to man."

But in this respect *Walden* is a notably different text from "Civil Disobedience" though both works begin, as it were, in the social world, *Walden* retreats into the self while "Civil Disobedience" calls for resistance to the government. This change can be seen in the book's very structure, its transition from "Economy" to "Conclusion," from Concord and Thoreau's neighbors to the inwardness of self-discovery. A mood of withdrawal totally dominates the final pages, as Thoreau urges his readers to turn their backs on society and look inside themselves. "Be a Columbus to whole new continents and worlds within you," he exhorts, "opening new channels, not of trade, but of thought. . . . [E]xplore the private sea, the Atlantic and Pacific Ocean of [your] being alone." The ending contains some of the book's best-known aphorisms, most of which revolve around the sentiment that "every one [should] mind his own business, and endeavor to be what he was made." The image left is of a solitary individual pursuing his own development, cultivating his own consciousness, in utter indifference to the common good. Such an image is not only radically at odds with the tone of *Walden*'s beginning; it also amounts to a distorted—and reified—reflection of the laissez-faire individualist pursuing his private economic interest at the expense of the public welfare.

Thoreau's unwitting kinship with social behavior he deplores can also be seen in his effort to create a myth of his experience. As the narrative progresses, he seems to grow intent upon suppressing all traces of autobiography and treating his two years at the pond as a timeless and universal experience. The patterning of the book after the cycle of the seasons contributes to this sense of the mythological, as does perhaps even more strongly the almost purely metaphorical character of the "Conclusion." In contrast to the specificity of the opening chapter, which takes place in Concord, Massachusetts, in the year 1845, the ending is situated in no time and no physical location. Thoreau declares open war on history: after ridiculing the "transient and fleeting" doings of his contemporaries, he vows "not to live in this restless, nervous, bustling, trivial Nineteenth Century, but stand or sit thoughtfully while it goes by." The text's denial of history, its flight from Jacksonian America, paradoxically resembles the commodified mode of thought which Thoreau charges against his countrymen and which permits a Flint to perceive his fruits and vegetables as dollars. In an analogous way, Thoreau allows the mythic value of his Walden experiment to displace the actual circumstances of its occurrence. Moreover, his determination to empty his adventure of historical content replicates a basic feature of reified consciousness. As he himself has pointed out repeatedly, market society engenders a conflation of history with nature. By presenting its limited, time-bound conventions as eternal, the existing order in effect places itself outside time and beyond the possibility of change. Although Thoreau rigorously condemns his society's "naturalizing" of itself in this fashion, he can be charged with performing a version of the same process on his own life by erasing history from *Walden* and mythologizing his experiment at the pond.

IV

The privatizing and antihistorical tendencies which blunt *Walden*'s critical edge reappear in Thoreau's attempt to devise a conception of reading and writing as unalienated labor. He is obliged to seek such a formulation because as a maker of texts, a would-be reformer in literature, he encounters the same problem that his neighbors experience in their daily transactions as farmers, merchants, and workmen: he has to confront the specter of the marketplace. In this area too Thoreau's rebuttal to exchange embroils him in difficulties he is unable to overcome. Indeed, the two goals he sets himself as an author, to initiate civic reformation while resisting the exchange process, turn out to be so incompatible by the mid-nineteenth century as to render their attainment mutually exclusive.

Trade, Throeau keeps insisting, "curses every thing it handles; and though you trade in messages from heaven, the whole curse of trade attaches to the business." Anything that is done for money, including the effort to instruct mankind, to be a "messenger from heaven" as Thoreau desires, is compromised by that very fact. Of his brief experience as a schoolteacher, he observes: "As I did not teach for the good of my fellowmen, but simply for a livelihood, this was a failure." In *Walden* he regularly refers to his readers as students—"Perhaps these pages are more particularly addressed to poor students," he says as early as the second paragraph—and he clearly sees the threat of failure hanging over his writing unless he can circumvent exchange in his dealings with his audience.

Thoreau regards life and presence, two qualities nullified by the capitalist market, as fundamental to his efficacy as an author-legislator. In censuring philanthropists, he says that their error is to distribute money rather than spending themselves. "Be sure to give the poor [i.e., poor students] the aid they most need, though it be your example which leaves them far behind." When he introduces himself on the first page as *Walden's* narrator, he emphasizes his own determination to retain the "I" or the self in his writing, to speak in the first person, and he adds that he requires of every writer "a simple and sincere account of his own life, and not merely what he has heard of other men's lives." This conception of literature as synonymous with life and the person recurs throughout the book, for example, when Thoreau states of the written word that it "is the work of art nearest to life itself. It may be translated into every language, and not only be read but actually breathed from all human lips." But if words have to be alive to "inspire" the reader, there are two senses in which exchange turns them into dead letters and kills the text. Since the cost of a thing is the amount of life expended for it, the book as commodity becomes an instrument of death like any item sold on the market. It also suffers an internal demise, commodification destroying literature's "bloom" just as surely as it blights the fruits and flowers on Flint's farm.

The literary work as article of exchange and the author as tradesman was the accepted state of affairs when Thoreau wrote *Walden*. As Tocqueville noted after his visit to America, the aristocratic domain of letters had become in democratic-capitalist society "the trade of literature." Thoreau, who claims to want "the flower and the fruit of a man, that some fragrance be wafted from him to me, and some ripeness flavor our intercourse," views the situation of literary culture with dismay. The books read and written by his countrymen, he feels, are not literature at all but commodities with the impoverished nature of commodities. Singularly lacking in either fragrance or flavor, they are fit only to be consumed by "those who, like cormorants and ostriches, can digest" any sort of foodstuff. To Thoreau, they are simply one more piece of merchandise in the unending stream of commerce which connects "the desperate city" to "the desperate country"; and like the huckleberries transported to the Boston market from the country's hills, they lose their most essential qualities in transit. "Up comes the cotton, down goes the woven cloth; up comes the silk, down goes the woolen; up comes the books, down goes the wit that writes them." Popular writers are "the machines to provide this provender," Thoreau contends, evoking his characterizations of both the huckleberry and the laboring man, and his neighbors are "the machines to read it." He proceeds to deliver a lengthy diatribe against fashionable literature and the public that devours it "with unwearied gizzard," concluding with the statement that "this sort of gingerbread is baked daily and more sedulously than pure wheat or rye-and-Indian in almost every oven, and finds a surer market."

In addition to changing the text into a commodity and taking away its life and essence, the marketplace endangers Thoreau's literary-civic enterprise because it encourages the reader in his addiction to mediation. Mediation, the substitution or replacement of one thing or person by another, is the heart and soul of the exchange process. In "Civil Disobedience" Thoreau disapproves of money, the medium of exchange, on precisely the grounds that it "comes between a man and his objects, and obtains them for him," thereby reducing his capacity for self-reliance. In *Walden* he states repeatedly that he wants the reader to obtain his objects by his own exertions (see his definition of a *"necessary of life"*). To allow the reader to accept Thoreau's experience as a substitute for his own would be the literary equivalent of the use of money. "I would not have any one adopt *my* mode of living on any account," he declares; rather, "I would have each one be very careful to find out and pursue his *own way*." Reading or studying something should never become a substitute for doing it, according to Thoreau, who expresses disdain for the "common course" of instruction whereby the student (or reader) is required "to study chemistry, and not learn how his bread is made, or mechanics, and not learn how it is earned." " 'But,' " he continues, anticipating a probable critic,

> "you do not mean that the students should go to work with their hands instead of their heads?" I do not mean that exactly, but I mean something which he might think a good deal like that; I mean that they should not *play* life, or *study* it merely, while the community supports them at this expensive game, but earnestly *live* it from beginning to end. How could youths better learn to live than by at once trying the experiment of living?

As Thoreau also points out, those who make a habit of depending on others through exchange and the division of labor court the risk of not being able to use their heads at all. "No doubt another *may* also think for me; but it is not therefore desirable that he should do so to the exclusion of my thinking for myself."

The reader who lets another do his thinking or his acting for him is a reader whose consciousness has been reified. He reacts to the words on the printed page with the same passivity and sense of noninvolvement as he feels in bowing to social reality. Most readers, in Thoreau's view, are in exactly this position; they limit themselves to books meant for deficient intellects and children and so "dissipate their faculties in what is called easy reading." To read in this feeble way, without exerting one's mind or relying on oneself, is merely to be confirmed in one's present condition. "Easy reading," like the writing which elicits it, obviously cannot promote the spirit of independence Thoreau seeks to nurture as the author of *Walden*.

Thoreau's task as a writer-reformer accordingly requires him to make a book which is not a commodity. To spare *Walden* the fate of the huckleberry, he has to ensure that like the pond it contains "no muck" and is "too pure to have a market value." He also has to find some way for the reader to eliminate mediation and achieve independence in his own right. And here again Thoreau has recourse to the civic humanist ideal of husbandry for his solution. He links authorship and agriculture and portrays both the artist and his audience as figurative husbandmen, extricating *Walden* from the marketplace by means of metaphor.

In "The Bean-Field" Thoreau draws a sustained comparison between composing a text and planting a crop. He likens himself at his hoe to "a plastic artist in the dewy and crumbling sand," and he speaks of "making the yellow soil express its summer thought in bean leaves and blossoms rather than in wormwood and piper and millet grass, making the earth say beans instead of grass." The writer as metaphorical farmer remains outside the exchange process and never deals in commodities because he never sells his crop for money. His text, which never reaches the Boston market, preserves its effectiveness as a living expression of his individuality.

Thoreau also depicts the reader as a laborer "of the hands" and contrasts the toil of reading *Walden* with the "easy reading" suitable to popular literature. He claims that the diligent student who sits alone with his books throughout the day and late into the night is "at work in *his* field, and chopping in *his* woods, as the farmer is in his." Such strenuous intellectual exertion is the price of comprehending *Walden,* which requires a "heroic reader" to emulate its heroic author. "The heroic books, even if printed in the character of our mother tongue, will always be in a language dead to degenerate times; and we must *laboriously* seek the meaning of each word and line, conjecturing a larger sense than common use permits out of what wisdom and valor and generosity we have" (italics added). The reader as symbolic farmer, tasked more by *Walden*'s intricacies than by "an exercise which the customs of the day esteem," triumphs over mediation by having the same "laborious" experience at his desk that Thoreau has at the pond. Reading *Walden* becomes figuratively identical with being at Walden, a discipline in the mental self-reliance which enables one, or so Thoreau believes, to penetrate the "veil of reification."

The qualification is in order because in metaphorizing reading and writing as activities outside history and the marketplace Thoreau disregards the realities of the text's evolution and his relation to the public. History forcibly enters *Walden* in the changes and additions made between the first draft and the published version, changes stretching over a period of nearly ten years. J. Lyndon Shanley, who has done the most thorough study of the original draft, finds that Thoreau enlarged the second half of the manuscript far more than the first, adding "more to the account of his life in the woods than to his criticism of contemporary ways," and that his major revisions were intended to emphasize the cycle of the seasons. The development *within* the text, in other words, corresponds to a development *outside* the text, a shift in attitude suggesting a deepening estrangement from the social realm. Thoreau seems to have suffered a crisis of confidence in the likelihood of civic reform and the idea of his writing as a means of instigating it. Besides the addition of the "Conclusion," none of which appeared in the first draft, one change in particular is unequivocal in suggesting his disenchantment with the role of educator-legislator. In both versions he speaks of planting in his readers the seeds of sincerity, truth, and simplicity, to "see if they will not grow in this soil." But missing from the original manuscript is the sentence which comes next in the book: "Alas! I said this to myself; but now another summer is gone, and another, and another, and I am obliged to say to you, Reader, that the seeds which I planted, if indeed they *were* the seeds of those virtues, were wormeaten or had lost their vitality, and so did not come up."

Between 1846, when he began *Walden,* and 1854, when he completed it, Thoreau had good reason to lose confidence in the viability of his civic aspirations. "Civil Disobedience" (1849) and *A Week on the Concord and Merrimack Rivers* (1849) had been published in that time; the first elicited no reaction whatsoever from the public, and the second has been described as "one of the most complete failures in literary history." In the final version of *Walden* Thoreau himself alludes to the discouraging reception of his earlier work. He tells the story of an Indian who came to Concord to sell baskets but learned to his chagrin that the inhabitants did not want to buy any. The Indian wrongly supposed that he had done his part by making the baskets, "and then it would be the white man's to buy them. He had not discovered," comments Thoreau,

> that it was necessary for him to make it worth the other's while
> to buy them, or at least make him think that it was so, or to
> make something else which it would be worth his while to buy.

> I too had woven a kind of basket of delicate texture, but I had
> not made it worth any one's while to buy them. Yet not the
> less, in my case, did I think it worth my while to weave them,
> and instead of studying how to make it worth men's while to
> buy my baskets, I studied rather how to avoid the necessity of
> selling them.

The "kind of basket" woven by Thoreau prior to *Walden* was of course *A Week,* a book which sold so poorly, as he reveals in a journal entry for 1853, that he was obliged to take possession of "706 copies out of an edition of 1000." He confides to the journal, and the bravado does not hide his own feelings of hurt and vexation, "I believe that this result is more inspiring and better for me than if a thousand had bought my wares. It affects my privacy less and leaves me freer."

Under the market system, there is no way for an author to exert influence to a significant degree without attracting a popular audience. If a book never reaches Boston, it is not likely to have much impact there. The influential writers praised by Thoreau enjoyed an "advantage" that was unavailable to him in the United States in the middle of the nineteenth century: the advantage of patronage by kings, noblemen, and warriors. Thoreau is caught in a contradiction of his own and history's devising: while he craves the authority of a founder, he refuses to view his text as a commodity and to accept "the necessity of selling" it. The failures of "Civil Disobedience" and *A Week* strengthen his antimarket resolution, but at the same time they force him to retreat from his ambition to reform the polity. Since he cannot shape popular opinion without large sales, he effectively abandons his civic project by striving to make *Walden* a difficult text at which the reader has to labor—hence a text which is inaccessible to the great majority of the public. "It is a ridiculous demand which England and America make," he writes in the "Conclusion," "that you shall speak so that they can understand you." And he goes on to voice defiant satisfaction that his own pages "admit of more than one interpretation," approximating the obscurity of the Walden ice. At this point Thoreau's celebration of figurative husbandry has become indistinguishable from the modernist credo of textual complexity, even incomprehensibility. The first draft of *Walden* was "Addressed to my Townsmen," but the last, colored by disappointment, seeks to exclude the many and narrow its appeal to a "fit audience, though few."

Thoreau worked five years longer on *Walden* than he had originally intended. Expecting a success with his first book, he hoped to bring out the second as early as 1849; copies of *A Week* included the announcement that *Walden* would be published shortly. But when it became evident that *A Week* was not selling, his publishers refused to issue *Walden,* and Thoreau spent five additional years revising and refining it. Since neither *A Week* nor the first draft of *Walden* is a masterpiece, this brief account of Thoreau's publishing difficulties suggests some final ironies of history. Insofar as *Walden* does "transcend" the age of Jackson, does rise above its historical moment as a consequence of its excellence as an artwork, it does so precisely because of the particular nineteenth-century circumstances under which it reached print. Its transcendence of history is rooted in the conditions of its production—its *belated* production—as a commodity to be marketed by publishers. And still more: there is the additional irony that *Walden* is its own most effective reply to Thoreau's denigrations of commercial enterprise. One need not even point out that the values of brotherhood and love, values conspicuously absent from *Walden,* are inextricably bound up with the principle of "exchange." On strictly aesthetic grounds, the text disputes the contention that "trade curses every thing it handles." Far from impairing the quality of *Walden,* commercial considerations conspired to make it a better work. *Walden* is the one undeniably great book Thoreau ever wrote, thanks in part to the operation of the marketplace.

Thoreau's Dawn and the Lake School's Night

Robert Weisbuch

A perfect earliness would be free of influence, and its literary statement would eschew allusion and all debate with other texts. The earliest author would be in immediate relation to Nature, in which, as Bergson tells us, no negative exists. One foot planted on the first grounds, the other on that ephemeral Ground of Spirit from which Nature spontaneously arises, the colossus of dawn would acknowledge nothing alien with which to bicker.

Such an uninfluenced earliness is Thoreau's goal, and he begins *Walden* by a bombardment of earliness images. He will write in the first person for "it is, after all, always the first person that is speaking." That is, he will speak truly, not just *in* but *as* the first person. He will hear no other voices, least those of elders, for age "has not profited so much as it has lost." He will write for "poor students" who must rely on their own experience for "if I have any experience which I think valuable, I am sure to reflect that this my Mentors said nothing about." Not to "*play* life, or *study* it merely," youth must "earnestly *live* it from beginning to end," where study would afford no authentic beginning from which to set out. The first person's only mentor, the one respected elder, is that "elderly dame," Nature, who "can tell me the original of every fable, and on what fact every one is founded, for the incidents occurred when she was young."

To be at the source of myth, "at the fountain head of day" with the "old settler and original proprietor" of Walden, "who tells me stories of old time and of new eternity": this is the only influence Thoreau will accept.

From *American Literature and British Influence in the Age of Emerson.* © 1986 by the University of Chicago. University of Chicago Press, 1986.

Thoreau locates a Walden spun out of the self's morning, "when I am awake and there is dawn in me," a place "to front only the essential facts of life." And like the actual frontiersman/backwoodsman, he moves forward to move backward, though in his act of cultural undoing he moves not at all. With no great interest in the actual west or the factual frontier, Thoreau temporizes the spatial promise. For him, as Edwin Fussell writes, "it was far more agreeable to step backward in time, while remaining in the same place." He wishes to be prelapsarian at a Walden "already in existence" perhaps "on that spring morning when Adam and Eve were driven out of Eden." It is time before time and scope beyond all space.

It is an impossibility. "I am not aware that any man has ever built on the spot which I occupy," Thoreau boasts. "Deliver me from a city built on the site of a more ancient city, whose materials are ruins, whose gardens cemeteries." Yet earlier he had confessed that his hoeing "disturbed the ashes of unchronicled nations." This is an act of recovery, but it shows that the New World is old even if the nation is young; and America in any case is busy refusing what youth it truly possesses. Nature's scope is ignored in favor of a going-indoors. "The nation itself, with all its so-called internal improvements, which, by the way, are all external and superficial" is "an unwieldy and overgrown establishment, cluttered with furniture." Even those unencumbered by an admiration for false improvements must front history and their postheroic moment. Elsewhere, traveling to Concord, N.H., Thoreau confesses, "We found that the frontiers were not this way any longer. This generation has come into the world fatally late for some enterprises."

The very vocation of writer prevents primacy. Thoreau's first and final dawn is by definition pre- and post-linguistic as it is before and beyond usual consciousness. As Eric Sundquist argues, its only expression would be an *ur* language from "an Eden at the outset of the history of rhetoric, . . . like the speech of a lost God." And in *The Maine Woods,* Thoreau admits sadly, "The poet's, commonly, is not a logger's path, but a woodman's. The logger and the pioneer have preceded him like John the Baptist: eaten the wild honey, it may be, but the locusts also." For his ease, the poet sacrifices priority and the wild.

Thoreau may wish "not to live in this restless, nervous, bustling, trivial Nineteenth Century, but stand or sit thoughtfully while it goes by"; he cannot. Bedeviled by an enforced lateness, Thoreau's rage at any chosen lateness invades his dawn wonder. "This hostility affects him," Charles Feidelson, Jr., writes. "His writing, explicitly or by implication, is always polemic and never, as he doubtless would wish, blandly indifferent to the assumptions of the enemy. Thoreau knows that earliness can become American blather, knows, as Stanley Cavell puts it, "that we are not free, not whole, and not new, and we know this, and are on a downward path because of it." But that means only "that the present is a task and a discovery, not a period of America's privileged history."

Earliness will be an act of will enabled by an acknowledgement of age, one's personal lateness and not alone the nation's or the nineteenth century's: "I long ago lost a hound, a bay horse, and a turtledove, and am still on their trail." But Thoreau's hoeing can renew the lost earliness. If writing is itself notice of a separation from the booming Eternal Now (and it is: "The volatile truth of our words should continually betray the inadequacy of the residual statement"), Thoreau will take measures against a too careful appearance of order to stress extra-vagance rather than unity. Finally, as a self-reward, he will melt his structure of words into the seasonal cycle, and then he will surpass nature to create eternal spring. If his very words come out of a language with a history, he will shed their habitual meanings and drive them etymologically back to their origins, not *OED* origins but "a larger sense than common use permits out of what wisdom and valor and generosity we have." If Thoreau is drawn to acknowledge the century's issues and disciplines, these too will be treated to his extra-vagant etymology, as when economy becomes "the cost of a thing" and cost "the amount of what I will call life which is required to be exchanged for it, immediately or in the long run." If he is not as poor a student as he would wish, then he will quote approvingly only from the earliest books from classical and oriental places, eastward, where the sun rises; and his quotings will be signs of confluence, not influence, for "I gaze upon as fresh a glory" as the Egyptian or Hindoo philosopher, "since it was I in him that was then so bold" as to raise "a corner of the veil from the statue of the divinity" just as "it is he in me that now reviews the vision." And if Thoreau must debate and if argument confesses intrusion, if the voice of wonder, epic celebration, and biblical prophecy must sometimes give way to the satirist's thrust, then that voice will be toned as the rustic churl's. Northrop Frye tells us that such a character, whose name connotes the argiculturally early, refuses "the mood of festivity" in comic narratives. Usually we do not like him. But, Frye notes, "The more ironic the comedy, the more absurd the society, and an absurd society may be condemned by, or at least contrasted with, a character that we may call the plain dealer, an outspoken advocate of a kind of moral norm who has the sympathy of the audience." Just so, Thoreau cries, "Simplicity, simplicity, simplicity!" at his "restless, nervous, bustling, trivial Nineteenth Century." In all, if he cannot be prelinguistic and totemic really, he can be so figuratively and drive back time a little bit at least by calling his writing notchings on a stick. Having accepted the latecoming status of woodman in that passage in *The Maine Woods,* Thoreau suddenly makes a choice of what had seemed an inevitability: "not only for strength, but for beauty, the poet must, from time to time," (and there is a pun here on the imaginative capacity for travel in time) "travel the logger's path and the Indian's trail, to drink at some new and more bracing fountain of the Muses, far in the recesses of the wilderness."

Most largely, as many commentators have noticed, Thoreau secedes from an America that, in its lateness, has lost itself. But he secedes by reenacting the American separation from England. He takes up his "abode in the woods," he reports, "by accident, . . . on Independence Day, or the Fourth of July 1845," a by-accident suggesting not meaninglessness but unplanned and thereby significant coincidence, as the double naming of the day implies. That is, Thoreau refuses the official nation for the American *patria.* Speaking of tea, coffee, and milk, the availability of which his visitor John Field considered a chief American advantage, Thoreau replies, "But the only true America is that country where you are at liberty to pursue such a mode of life as may enable you to do without these." The accusations he must rebut—that he is neglecting his social responsibilities, that he will become a heathen, that his venture is wildly impractical—recall the seventeenth-century British animadversions against the colonists; and his planting activities recapitulate the Puritan settlement.

I would add to this commonplace a simple emphasis on what Thoreau is seceding from it: it is England, or an America gone specifically English. England as a term in *Walden* stands simply and consistently for that which is too premeditated and overcultivated (like English hay) and for that which is too circumscribed (like the hunting grounds of English noblemen or the official English holidays implying the scheduled limiting of joys that should be daily). England stands for that which is decadent ("The government of the world I live in was not framed, like that of Britain, in after-dinner conversations over the wine") or exploitative ("England, which is the great workhouse of the world"). England has nothing to tell us: "as for England, almost the last significant scrap of news from that quarter" (notice the employment of Sydney Smith's word from the phrase "In the four quarters of the globe, who reads an American book?") "was the revolution of 1649." But America's own revolution has done nothing to halt the infiltration of British lateness. Our workers live in conditions "every day more like that of the English," and Irish John Field stands for an America still deeply colonial in "thinking to live by some derivative old country mode in this primitive new country."

Thoreau makes portable the idea of America to take it away from that Englamerica, the existent America that is a traitor to its own earliness. Part of that removal is explicitly literary, Thoreau's attempt to separate from English romanticism. And in that rebellion, the idea of the Wild, which elsewhere Thoreau figures with the fruitful nervousness of a civilized thinker, becomes an unambiguous value.

II

On the title page of the first edition appears, in bold capitals, this sentence: I DO NOT PROPOSE TO WRITE AN ODE TO DEJECTION, BUT TO BRAG AS LUSTILY AS CHANTICLEER IN THE MORNING, STANDING ON HIS ROOST, IF ONLY TO WAKE MY NEIGHBORS UP. Coleridge is Thoreau's chosen opposite, specifically the night waking poet of "Dejection: An Ode." He is the insomniac in rooms who looks out on an ill-omened moon through too literary eyes that have lost the creative power to unite nature and mind in an act of godly joy. And he is everyway rejected as a model by an American who situates himself outdoors not only at dawn but at the dawn of his opponent's home literature. Chanticleer is a type-name for a rooster, but it is Chaucer who is implied by the name in this literary sentence; and, like Thoreau, Chaucer was another poet of national earliness who had to battle foreign influence. Coleridge's fatigued self-pity marks a long English decline from Chaucer's morning cheer. It is Thoreau's New England neighbors who are to be awakened, but clearly neighbor England, in its originary spirit, is to be saved from its own lateness as well.

Why Coleridge as the negative English representative? I have implied one reason. The most self-disappointed of romantic personae, one who, even when he proclaims an imaginative faith at ode's end, sees himself barred from active participation in that faith, would be a large and likely target. Who better than the author of "Dejection" could be accused of exporting to America an attitude that would cause "lives of quiet desperation"? The man who complains that the "dull sobbing draft" of melancholic weather upon his Aeolian lute makes him wish that romantic emblem of sounding spirit "mute" announces a death-wish. Thoreau wishes to be awake and all-natural while Coleridge accuses himself of choosing "by abstruse research to steal / From my own nature all the natural man." Coleridge chronicles a lateness–decline within the course of his own life, aside from English literary history. He is set off against a man who self-approvingly chooses to imitate both an unthinking natural animal and a god in order to initiate a world.

But of course there is more to Thoreau's choice of Coleridge for a specific rejection. This is not so plainly a case of kicking a good man when he is down. Indeed Thoreau does trivialize the ode. The night of self-pity is spectacularly transformed, first when Coleridge refuses his own melodramatic comparison to Lear to see himself as merely "a little child / Upon a lonesome wild, / Not far from home, but she hath lost her way"; and then in an act of outgoing generosity as he wishes for the "Dear Lady" that inner joy of which he has become incapable. Hard honesty and a love for the other which survives despair may mark more of a recovery than the poet knows or owns. Indeed, Coleridge's speaker finally enacts Thoreau's own dictum, "We may waive just so much care of ourselves as we honestly bestow elsewhere," another of the poem's implications that Thoreau's allusion discounts.

Thoreau strikes at Coleridge not because Coleridge is a good man down but because Coleridge is a giant keeping him under, an influential poet and thinker whom Thoreau so resembles in many points that differences need to be dramatized for Thoreau to make his own home in an American woods.

Most largely, as Lawrence Buell notes, Coleridge is credited with the importation to America of European pantheisms that emphasize "a metaphysical correspondence between nature and spirit," and it is precisely this sense that Emerson named Thoreau's best gift, the drawing of "universal law from the single fact." Further, Coleridge everywhere stresses that "priority of relation over substance," which Charles Feidelson Jr. sees as vital to Thoreau's art of perception. Neither Coleridge nor Thoreau consistently believes in a plain projectivism whereby the self utterly produces the out-there, but both can be drawn to such a view. The Coleridge who writes in "Dejection"

> O Lady! we receive but what we give,
> And in our life alone does Nature live:
> Ours is her wedding garment, our her shroud!
>
> . . . .
>
> Ah! from the soul itself must issue forth
> A light, a glory, a fair luminous cloud
> Enveloping the earth—

is perfectly met by the Thoreau who argues that architectural beauty "has gradually grown from within outward, out of the necessities and character of the indweller, who is the only builder—out of some unconscious truthfulness, and nobleness, without ever a thought for the appearance." And

Thoreau again, perhaps via Emerson, sounds the Coleridgean idea when he devalues the making of beautiful objects by calling it "far more glorious to carve and paint the very atmostphere through which we look, which morally we can do."

Finally, Coleridge and Thoreau share, in James McIntosh's words, a "sense of nature as one, as alive, and as the aggregate of things," a sense generally romantic. But it is named most succinctly by Coleridge in "The Eolian Harp," where he glorifies "the one Life within us and abroad, / Which meets all motion and becomes its soul," and Thoreau takes up Coleridge's image when he writes of distant sound as creating "a vibration of the universal lyre."

Yet McIntosh goes on to insist that "Thoreau and his European counterparts are romantics, not Orphists or Parsees or Buddhists, partly because they share a more or less open awareness of their separation from nature, however much they may desire to be at home in it." Here the two writers begin to differ. McIntosh's generalization is importantly valid, but consider that no other romantic poet stresses depressive isolation so consistently as Coleridge and that Thoreau's isolation issues in self-sufficient joy. "Alone, alone, all, all alone, / Alone on a wide, wide sea" seems Coleridge's motto everywhere. The mariner, Christabel, and the personae of such lyrics as "Dejection," "Frost at Midnight," and "This Lime-tree Bower My Prison" victimized by a self-absorption pictured as literal seclusion. Granted, this is only a nadir from which many of Coleridge's speakers rise in such acts of outgoing love as we mentioned in "Dejection." In solitude, that is, they may connect to the "one Life" that affords more of a communal sense than any crowd might. But it is only this affirming paradox that Thoreau adapts in his chapter "Solitude": "I have a great deal of company in my house; especially in the morning, when nobody calls. . . . God is alone,—but the devil, he is far from being alone; he sees a great deal of company; he is legion." In "The Eolian Harp" Coleridge finally denigrates and refuses as unholy his pantheistic vision of the "one Life," that sense of an expanded society among nature, man, and God that Thoreau adopts to people his seclusion. And given Thoreau's version of a Coleridge reduced to mere dejection by the lyre of another occasion, Thoreau's affirmation of his own company again accuses Coleridge of an unnecessary despair.

Coleridge as the English writer is not only night-sad but over-civilized and every way barred from the spontaneity that is the only good. Thoreau takes the extraordinary measure of repeating his motto in "Where I Lived, and What I Lived For" as if to guarantee our awareness of these implications. He prefaces it by the sentence, "The present was my next experiment of this kind, which I purpose to describe more at length, for convenience, putting the experience of two years into one." "The present" may mean only the present experiment but it also may mean that the experiment of Walden was an attempt to live utterly in the present: as he writes earlier, "to stand on the meeting of two eternities, the past and future, which is precisely the present moment; to toe that line." Given that Coleridge's "Dejection" is named once more in the next sentence, Thoreau's "present" and the packing of two years into one are in vivid distinction to the lassitude of loose moments with which the Ode opens and to the general sense of an irrevocable Fall throughout.

Immediate participation is the claim of the motto itself. "I do not propose to write . . . but to brag as lustily as Chanticleer in the morning." Of course, Thoreau *is* writing, but, as we have noted, *Walden* is arranged so as to avoid anything like the tight structure of an ode, with a simulated and-that-brings-to-mind spontaneity rather than the scene, meditation, in-itial-scene-transformed movement of Coleridge's poem, much less the rig-orous ordering of Coleridge's philosophical writings. Bragging is vocal, part of an earlier, oral mode of transmission, and it is early too in refusing the sublimating restraints upon the ego of a Christian-civilized humility. By such means is Coleridge made all too much a poet. (Thoreau mentions "Ode to Dejection" on one other occasion. In his journal, he describes how a tree may be made more beautiful by a diseased swelling of its tissue. "Beautiful scarlet sins they may be . . . This gall is the tree's 'Ode to Dejection.' " This is to give compliment to Coleridge's poem as creating beauty out of personal malaise, but the trope implicitly defines Coleridge's mood as an abnormal, insect-infested disease. He elsewhere calls "Art itself a gall." More generally, then, Coleridge's Ode simply signifies high art, an injury to inexpressive nature but an injury that is also a benefit. In the context of *Walden,* however, where sublimated acts, including high art, are called into most skeptical question, the paradox of beauty through disrup-tion is removed, and the Ode as the incursion of a diseased art into nature is a gall pure and simple. This is so especially in regard to the motto.) And in his motto Thoreau is libidinally potent, as he brags "lustily," a word that might mean simply "with exuberance" were it not connected to Chau-cer's rooster. In "Dejection," contrarily, Coleridge accuses himself of gen-eral impotence and is apparently barred (as we know he was factually) from the "Dear Lady" he blesses at ode's end just as he is barred from the source of inner joy he celebrates in absentia. This, Thoreau implies, is where the sublimations of civilized life get you, as he leagues in preference with a barnyard animal.

This is the ultimate difference to which Thoreau's allusion points. The poet of lateness recalls a vision that he no longer can experience internally, much less enact to transform the world. Thoreau, as the bard of the early hour when all is possible, wishes to literalize vision as it has never been made literal before. "When one man has reduced a fact of the imagination to be a fact to his understanding, I foresee that all men will at length establish their lives on that basis." From beans will derive a global village of vision, as Thoreau accepts Coleridge's differentiated terms (the imagination is allied to Reason as a self-referential totality transcending the secondary imagination's Understanding in *Aids to Reflection,* a book Thoreau owned) but demands an actualization of the divine I AM on the most common and available grounds imaginable, democratic American earth. The poet of lateness can barely imagine his imagination; he can recall it only. The bard of dawn lives out his now-forming imagination from July 4, 1845, forward "about a mile and a half south of the village of Concord" by Walden Pond.

And yet Thoreau does not dismiss Coleridge; he includes the English poet as an item within his emotional range. Coleridge is the poet of night waking owls. "Tu-whit! Tu-whoo!" they cry at the beginning of "Christabel" and "The owlet's cry / Came loud—and hark, again! loud as before" at the beginning of "Frost at Midnight." Thoreau hears in the owls' cries at Walden the words *"Oh-o-o-o-o that I had never been bor-r-r-r-n!"* Thoreau grudgingly acknowledges that they speak to one of nature's many truths, "the stark twilight and unsatisfied thoughts which all have" and thus have their place at a Walden that can afford even despair by placing it within an encyclopedia of other sounds. As McIntosh notes, Thoreau "generally prefers not to exhibit his acquaintance with Wordsworth and Coleridge, Carlyle and Goethe" and so he attributes literary owls to Ben Jonson, while reproducing nearly Coleridge's (admittedly Shakespeare's as well, in the song from *Love's Labour's Lost)* "Tu-whit Tu-whoo" in his next sentence. But when he speaks of the owls' meaning, it is the poet of lateness he attacks. They are "expressive of a mind which has reached the gelatinous mildewy stage of all healthy and courageous thought. It reminded me of ghouls and idiots and insane howlings." Yet the owl has its place at Walden and Thoreau can employ Coleridge for incentive. In "Christabel," recall, "the owls have awakened the crowing cock," though Coleridge's rooster crows "drowsily," acknowledging English night, while Thoreau's owl makes Coleridge's night of despair itself "a more dismal and fitting day."

III

And now another dawn springs of midnoon, as I wish to unsay, or at least complicate my claim. Coleridge is not the leading figure for England in *Walden,* but only the most overt. Coleridge stands in for the more powerful influence of Wordsworth, as Thoreau makes Wordsworth's claim for the "abundant recompense" of mature age tantamount to Coleridge's dejection.

Thoreau clearly pairs the two, and both together represent what he sees as the going idea of literature itself. "This is my lake country," he says of the ponds surrounding Walden. And later, in an 1859 journal entry, "There are poets of all kinds and degrees, little known to each other. The Lake School is not the only or the principal one." Granted, Coleridge is nominating a sleazy muskrat-hunter as yet another poet of sorts, but the entry assumes an agreement that the Lake School is generally thought to define poetry, or at least poetry of natural enthusiasm.

But Wordsworth is not merely an afterthought to be included with Coleridge; it is Wordsworth more. McIntosh quotes an early poem by Thoreau to "surmise that Thoreau professed so vocally his intention not to write an Ode to Dejection in *Walden* because he was personally familiar with the feelings evoked and the questions raised in Coleridge's poem."

> *The Poet's Delay*
> In vain I see the morning rise,
> In vain observe the western blaze,
> Who idly look to other skies,
> Expecting life by other ways.
>
> Amidst such boundless wealth without,
> I only still am poor within,
> The birds have sung their summer out,
> But still my spring does not begin.

But the poem bears a much closer resemblance to the second stanza of a different ode, Wordsworth's "Intimations of Immortality."

> The Rainbow comes and goes,
> And lovely is the Rose,
> The moon doth with delight
> Look round her when the heavens are bare;
> Waters on a starry night
> Are beautiful and fair;
> The sunshine is a glorious birth.
> But yet I know, where'er I go,
> That there hath past away a glory from the earth.

The spiritless praising of an animated nature and a guilty sense that the self's preoccupations, in Wordsworth's phrase, "the season wrong" is imitated closely in Thoreau's poem; and McIntosh himself affirms that "for nineteenth-century New Englanders, Wordsworth was *the* poet of nature" and that Wordsworth's Ode was the single poem "that seems to have affected Thoreau most strongly." It is the figure of Wordsworth, I believe, beyond any single poem, that engages Thoreau, for Americans tend to think in terms of human representatives rather than texts, in confronting what is English.

Wordsworth appears throughout *Walden,* though always incognito. Like Wordsworth, Thoreau worries that the world is too much with us, and he too recommends not augmentations but a purificatory shedding as the means of hope. Like Wordsworth, who saves his awe for the simple individual who is part of a landscape and who hates the crowdings of cities, Thoreau writes, "We live thick and are in each other's way, and stumble over one another, and I think that we thus lose some respect for one another." Like Wordsworth with his leech-gatherer, Thoreau personifies the grandeur of simplicity in a deliberately unheroic-seeming man, the Canadian woodchopper. Thoreau affords his ideal man a more detailed and convincing facticity and allows himself to wonder whether "to suspect him of a fine poetic consciousness or of stupidity." But the woodchopper, like Wordsworth's old man and his other vagabonds, exemplifies that absence of self-consciousness and the concomitant providential assurance that Thoreau directly advises when he writes, "I think that we may safely trust a good deal more than we do. We may waive just so much care of ourselves as we honestly bestow elsewhere." Like Wordsworth too, Thoreau locates a more supernaturally tinged kind of simplicity in the child. Of such as Wordsworth's "best Philosopher," "filling from time to time his 'humorous stage,' " Thoreau writes, "Children, who play life, discern its true laws and relations more clearly than men."

These are not piecemeal similarities. For both writers, they contribute to a program for earliness. More significantly, both writers travel through a spectrum of descriptions of earliness. This spectrum ranges in each between a love of earliness-as-nature so intense that the self is always seen as too late in relation to it and a love of earliness-as-preexistential vision in which earliest nature itself is too late to fulfill the demands of the imagination. There is a Wordsworth who frolics in a simple natural ecstacy and a more mystic Wordswroth who wishes to look upon natural objects with an eye so intense that object and eye surpass their material condition and we "become a living soul" that can "see into the life of things" ("Tintern

Abbey") and reads in a landscape "characters of the great Apocalypse" (*The Prelude*). Just so, in Fussell's felicitous phrase, "To the end, Thoreau seems undetermined whether he means to be on the frontier or beyond," with his final goal simple, essential living or the employment of that kind of living to achieve an inexplicable bliss of unity with the spirit-source.

As much as Wordsworth, Thoreau praises childhood from a position of privation, the vantage-point of adult loss. "I have always been regretting that I was not as wise as the day I was born," Thoreau writes in *Walden*. And his later journal entries that mourn a loss of power could as well quote directly from Wordsworth's crisis poems, as when he writes, "Once I was part and parcel of Nature; now I am observant of her." The famous sentence from *Walden,* "I long ago lost a hound, a bay horse, a turtle-dove, and am still on their trail," employs images that tease us to identify them while they clearly serve as emblems of a general loss. Just so, Wordsworth in the Intimations Ode confesses to "a Tree, of many, one, / A single field which I have looked upon," both of which speak "of something that is gone," the glory and the dream. And in these instances, natural images are employed to dramatize a loss of something not only natural but preternatural. There is a Thoreau who wishes "to walk even with the Builder of the universe," who "sometimes expected the Visitor who never comes," who speaks Plato-like of "the dark unfathomed mammoth cave of this world," who proclaims that "we are not wholly involved in Nature," and for whom "time is but the stream I go a-fishing in." Such statements lead to that anti-natural extreme epitomized in a journal entry from the period when *Walden* is being written.

> We soon get through with Nature. She excites an expectation which she cannot satisfy. The merest child which has rambled into a copsewood dreams of a wilderness so wild and strange and inexhaustible as Nature can never show him.

That same Thoreau directly quotes Wordsworth in an earlier journal: "Methinks my present experience is nothing; my past experience is all in all. . . . As far back as I can remember I have unconsciously referred to the experiences of a previous state of being. 'For life is a forgetting'; etc." He corresponds to the Wordsworth who finally finds not even the Alps sufficient to the human imagination, which is "A thousand times more beautiful than the earth / On which he dwells."

Like Wordsworth, Thoreau represents himself as a walker. His "favorite form," Buell argues, "is the romantic excursion." This natural dynamism is accompanied in both writers by a constant mental traveling between the poles of natural earliness and an earliness that is the ground of nature but is itself incorporeal, as any thing must be defined by what it is not. The characteristic tension in both writers is between idealist and naturalist urgings.

We could enlarge our list of similarities that, in part, bespeak Thoreau's acceptance of Wordsworth's teaching. We could discuss in each the mocking translation of economic terms into considerations of spiritual cash. We could emphasize in each the dramatizations of a childhood wildness which violates nature for a purpose. Or we could cite the recommendation of relaxed reception, Wordsworth's "wise passivity," throughout *Walden*. But it is more to our purpose, as it was to Thoreau's, to discover crucial differences.

First and simply, Thoreau most echoes Wordsworth or Coleridge when he speaks of his own insufficiencies and of Nature's, and *Walden* is predominantly an account of success, the self's ability to find significant life in the earliness of a capacious Nature. "Both place and time were changed, and I dwelt nearer to those parts of the universe and to those eras in history which had most attracted me." Second, although *Walden* is written in the past tense and McIntosh is technically right to attribute it to "a sense of remembered place," that is not the book's dominant effect. In such of Wordsworth's lyrics as "I Wandered Lonely as a Cloud," the imaginative memory does not merely recollect earlier experience but augments, completes, perfects it. That is not true of *Walden,* which carries us quasi-chronologically through a series of percepts that immediately become concepts. That Walden to which Thoreau attributes a prelapsarian existence is the Walden that he "in the First person" directly experiences.

The verb "experiences" leads to a third and underlying difference that Thoreau marks between himself and Wordsworth. In the Tintern Abbey lyric, Wordsworth is suprised to see "pastoral farms / Green to the very door; and wreaths of smoke / Sent up, in silence, from among the trees!" He imaginatively infers "vagrant dwellers in the houseless woods" whom he implicitly praises for a harmony achieved with nature. But Wordsworth himself is not one of them, just as, seated reflectively beneath a "dark sycamore," he is not immediately part of ever dynamic nature, "of sportive wood run wild": against that contrast, the rest of the poem must struggle toward an affirmation of age. Thoreau is himself one of those "vagrant dwellers." Just as Wordsworth's pastoral farms are "Green to the very door," Thoreau proclaims of his house, "No Yard! but unfenced Nature reaching up to your very sills." Whereas a civilized Wordsworth looks into nature and a remembered natural self, Thoreau locates himself there: "no gate—no front-yard,—and no path to the civilized world."

Thoreau enacts what Wordsworth contemplates. Again: both Thoreau and Wordsworth horizontalize the universe, find high meaning in low objects; but Wordsworth only in contemplation finds at the conclusion of the Intimations Ode that "the meanest flower that blows can give / Thoughts that do often lie too deep for tears" while Thoreau, wishing to know beans, actively cultivates them. Thoreau may allow for characters more primitive than himself, closer to "life near the bone where it is sweetest," such as the woodchopper, but primarily he is himself that Solitary Reaper whose song can inspirit a Wordsworth who is himself too late in time to sing it.

It is not simply that Thoreau describes nature far more particularly than Wordsworth. The claim is that he can be intimately, body-and-soul, amidst nature as the mature Wordsworth spiritually cannot be. When Wordsworth wishes in the Intimations Ode for a simple regression, when he attempts to return to the shores of the ocean of life and leap with the children in festival, the thought of that "Tree" intervenes and reveals the falseness of an adult Wordsworth galumphing about. Yet for the loss of that connection to nature occurs "abundant recompense." Even as a natural child, Wordsworth had felt the loss of an earlier All, and that sense of loss which led to spiritual realization educates him to the good of the present one. Distance from nature affords imaginative space for Faith, for the "philosophic mind" which best appreciates both nature and specifically human courage. Dawn is done but sunset promises a greater return to the state before and beyond time early or late.

For Thoreau, any loss of connection to nature is absolute loss. Men think they are wiser than children, "wiser by experience, that is, failure" and "with years I have grown more coarse and indifferent." Earliness is all, and the return which Wordsworth finally counts folly is exactly what Thoreau desires. "That man who does not believe that each day contains an earlier, more sacred, and auroral hour than he has yet profaned, has despaired of life, and is pursuing a descending and darkening way." As Charles Anderson succinctly puts it, "Thoreau's search to discover his ideal self becomes a quest to recover his lost youth in a second spring." But at his most optimistic, Thoreau contemplates no loss. It is getting earlier all the time.

From this perspective, Wordsworth's "abundant recompense" is hollow rationalization, and he, as much as Benjamin Franklin, is the target of ridicule when Thoreau continues his rhetoric of dawn by asking, "Who would not be early to rise, and rise earlier and earlier each successive day of his life, till he became unspeakably healthy, wealthy, and wise?" In all,

Thoreau accounts himself the worshipper of Hebe, "who had the power of restoring gods and men to the vigor of youth."

Of Hebe, Thoreau continues, "Wherever she came it was spring." His confessions of decay are confined to a thoroughly personal voice much subordinate in *Walden* to a self who microcosmically speaks for American possibility. Earliness is made all-portable, all-persistent. "Morning brings back the heroic ages." "Morning is when I am awake and there is dawn in me." The "Bhagvat Geeta" expresses a wisdom that should "be referred to a previous state of existence" and "the pure Walden water is mingled with the sacred water of the Ganges." A return to the early is no more difficult than the return of spring. If dawn is not immediately present, that is not because it is irrecoverably lost in an English past—Wordsworth's cultural implication, if we read his personal mythology as partly a social and historical one as well—but because it is yet to come in an American future. "I have never yet met a man who was quite awake." "We loiter in winter while it is already spring." "Only that day dawns to which we are awake. There is more day to dawn. The sun is but a morning star."

Thoreau vacillates cannily between envisioning Walden as the ultimate earliness, the final good in itself, and envisioning Walden as one of any number of paths to an atemporal good. The latter is his escape clause from too literal and didactic a claim. But he need not decide between the alternatives, for earliness is scope and scope makes everything possible. Walden may or may not be it, but Thoreau is after an attainable ultimacy available to the time of our earth. Such a belief makes of Wordsworth's beyond-sunset faith nothing more than fancy work upon Coleridge's plain dejection. Wordsworth tends to assign his natural intensity to childhood, his mysticism to mature thought (though, we need to add, that mature thought is informed by the earlier love of plain nature). Thoreau's paradox of the frontier, whereby he moves forward not to sunset but to sunrise and makes West East, refuses all ordinary temporality, including historical and personal aging. His prize term, "The Wild," brilliantly contains his nature-loving and his spirit-longing aspects, for it means not only "savage, primitive" but also "unconditioned."

Thus, in *Walden,* as Thoreau "rambles into higher and higher grass," the book's seasonal cycle becomes an increasing parabola spinning forward by running backward into the untamed. Thoreau's earliness is not in a place or at a time. "Any prospect of awakening or coming to life to a dead man makes indifferent all times and places." Material fact and spiritual law get transformed instantly, as by instinct, into each other so that earliness becomes less a condition or state than an activity. By its reverse dynamism, we spin ever more rapidly backward until we pass through a vortex of the beginning and through an earlier vortex before that and then an earlier. We must "rise earlier and earlier each successive day" for "each day contains an earlier, more sacred, and auroral hour"; and Thoreau's last sentence anticipates yet earlier beginnings as "the sun is but a morning star."

From Beaumont's picture of Peele Castle in a storm, Wordsworth learns that his early view of the castle as exampling "lasting ease, / Elysian quiet, without toil or strife" and, most, "silent Nature's breathing life" was pathetically blind. "But welcome fortitude, and patient cheer, / And frequent sights of what is to be borne!" Thoreau eschews Wordsworth's "humanised Soul," sees it as the spirit of defeat, and in his actualist American faith teaches of castles a different lesson: "If you have built castles in the air, your work need not be lost; that is where they should be. Now put the foundations under them." And that is why, for Thoreau, "Wordsworth is too tame for the Chippeway."

IV

[Elsewhere] I summarized Sacvan Bercovitch's persuasive theory of a major difference between Protestant theologies in Old and New England. Calvinism in Britain, however radical, always maintains a distinction between the city of God and the cities of man, a gap that New England was founded expressly to close. New England expects an attainable earthly paradise, an ending transformation of historical time into a life of spirit. Especially upon the failure of Cromwell's Commonwealth, Britain would treat with scepticism any such literalisms.

Once we add to this the far more recent and significant failure of human hope in the French revolution, we are a ways to explaining the differences between the Lake poets and Thoreau. The French disaster would teach a stern lesson on the consequences of confusing internal and individual redemption with political rebellion. For Coleridge and Wordsworth, the lesson only would reinforce a privatism, a scepticism toward the utopian, inherited from their culture. Contrarily, the success of the American revolution, though it might seem all to exclusively political to a mind like Thoreau's, could not but rekindle hope for an absolute merge of personal and national salvation. Wordsworth replaces his political dogmatism with personal recovery. Thoreau secedes from the America of fact to found no private domain, whatever Walden at first may seem, but to revive and live out what he calls "the only true America."

By that, we can account too for a final difference. It concerns the structuring of an audience. Coleridge and Wordsworth typically address a like-minded friend, often each other. The intimate tone creates a society of two in quiet defiance of the loveless crowd, which is the world at large. Thoreau takes a far more public stance, that of a Jeremiah haranguing his neighbors, all of them, the nation. It is conversation on one side of the Atlantic, conversion sermons on the other.

You don't live by what you say and what you say does not say far enough: what I described as the typical American critique of English romanticism suits this case. So too does that habit whereby the American, speaking as a national representative, makes the British writer whom he confronts representative as well. To Thoreau, Wordsworth and Coleridge are England, however much these writers themselves insisted on their separate, private country.

It is not surprising, then, that Thoreau's explicit commentaries on England chime with his implicit criticisms of Coleridge and Wordsworth. "The crop of *English* hay" (Thoreau's italic) "is carefully weighed, the moisture calculated" while the wilds produce "a rich and various crop unreaped by man." When he calls his field, and so *Walden,* "the connecting link between wild and cultivated fields" and "half-cultivated," he seems to compromise. But then "they were beans cheerfully returning to their wild and primitive state that I cultivated," and so earliness is retained, even furthered, and cultivation receives a backward definition.

Linear and historical time, English property, are undone in *Walden.* Thoreau's emphasis on dawn and earliness give special meaning to a jibe like "The government of the world I live in was not framed, like that of Britain, in after-dinner conversations over the wine." And in his role as the Salem merchant, peddling a "Celestial Empire" that refuses history's claims and reverses time's decay, Thoreau sells "purely native products . . . always in native bottoms."

Given that England is consistently equated with a public world decaying in its accumulations, with a materialism devoid of spirit and, even in its most visionary aspect, with the open despair of Coleridge and the desperate rationalizings of Wordsworth, and given that Walden is an explicitly American experiment, we are at first surprised to hear Thoreau halloo "Welcome, Englishmen! welcome, Englishmen! for I had had communication with that race." And we are as surprised when he links the two nations in despite in his final pages—"It is said that the British Empire is very large and respectable, and that the United States are a first-rate power"—and lectures John and Jonathan alike. But again we are in the midst of a deceptive compromise. We noted that Thoreau sees the public

America as having gone English. Indeed, when he welcomes Englishmen, Thoreau may as well mean village visitors, for he has relived the emigration from England in leaving citied New England for the wild. Despite independence, official America has been annexed to the British again.

But the English visit him, not he them. And as Salem merchant, Thoreau does not merely sell his goods, he "will export such goods as the country affords." If John and Jonathan are to save themselves, they will have to awake to a dawn, a sun, a morning that belongs to the wild, the west, American earliness. *Walden* is a counterannexation.

Chronology

1817	David Henry Thoreau born on July 12 at Concord, Massachusetts. (He later changed his name to Henry David.)
1828	Enters Concord Academy.
1833	Enters Harvard College.
1837	Graduates from Harvard. Begins teaching in the Concord School, but resigns when required to administer corporal punishment. Meets Emerson and begins writing his *Journal*.
1838	Starts a private school with his brother John. Gives his first public lecture at the Concord Lyceum.
1839	Canoe trip on the Concord and Merrimack rivers with John, described in *A Week on the Concord and Merrimack Rivers*.
1840	Publishes in the *Dial*, the new magazine of the Transcendentalists.
1841	Takes up residence at Emerson's home, as tutor and handyman.
1842	Thoreau's brother John dies of lockjaw after cutting his finger.
1843	Thoreau tutors in the family of Emerson's brother William, on Staten Island.
1844	Returns home, works at family's pencil-making business.
1845	Begins building a house on the banks of Walden Pond.
1846	First camping trip to the Maine woods. Arrested in Concord and jailed overnight for refusing to pay the poll tax to a government that supported slavery and waged an imperialist war against Mexico.
1847	Leaves Walden Pond and again moves in with the Emersons.
1849	Moves back to his father's house. *A Week on the Concord and Merrimack Rivers* and "Civil Disobedience" published. First visit to Cape Cod.
1850	Travels again to Cape Cod and then to Canada.
1853	Second trip to Maine.

1854   Publishes *Walden, or, Life in the Woods*. Delivers "Slavery in Massachusetts" lecture.

1855   Third journey to Cape Cod.

1856   Meets Walt Whitman in New York.

1857   Fourth visit to Cape Cod. Third trip to the Maine woods. Meets the abolitionist John Brown, who was hanged after a raid on Harper's Ferry.

1859   Delivers "A Plea for John Brown."

1860   Last camping excursion to Monadnock.

1861   Goes to Minnesota because of failing health.

1862   Thoreau dies of tuberculosis on May 6.

1874   Thoreau's body moved from Concord to Author's Ridge at Sleepy Hollow.

Contributors

Harold Bloom, Sterling Professor of the Humanities at Yale University, is the author of *The Anxiety of Influence, Poetry and Repression,* and many other volumes of literary criticism. His forthcoming study, *Freud: Transference and Authority,* attempts a full-scale reading of all of Freud's major writings. A MacArthur Prize Fellow, he is general editor of five series of literary criticism published by Chelsea House. During 1987–88, he was appointed Charles Eliot Norton Professor of Poetry at Harvard University.

Loren Eiseley has written books on evolution, anthropology, a biography of Francis Bacon, and several volumes of poetry. He was Benjamin Franklin Professor of Anthropology and the History of Science at the University of Pennsylvania.

George Sibley, writer, philosopher, and mountaineer, is the author of the forthcoming book *Timber in North America.*

Judith P. Saunders is Assistant Academic Dean at Marymount College.

Harold Hellenbrand teaches English at California State College in San Bernardino.

Ronald B. Shwartz, a Boston attorney, is former editor of *The University of Chicago Law Review.* His articles have appeared in *The Nation, The Wall Street Journal,* and *The Boston Globe.*

Joseph G. Kronick is Assistant Professor of English at Louisiana State University. He is the author of *American Poetics of History: From Emerson to the Moderns.*

Michael T. Gilmore teaches at Brandeis University. He has edited several books on colonial and nineteenth-century literature and is the author of *The*

Middle Way: Puritanism and Ideology in American Romantic Fiction, and *American Romanticism and the Marketplace.*

ROBERT WEISBUCH is Associate Professor of English at the University of Michigan. He is the author of *Emily Dickinson's Poetry* and *Atlantic Double-Cross: American Literature and British Influence in the Age of Emerson.*

Bibliography

Abbey, Edward. *Down the River.* New York: Dutton, 1982.

Anderson, Charles R. *The Magic Circle of Walden.* New York: Holt, Rinehart & Winston, 1968.

Bowling, Lawrence. "Thoreau's Social Criticism as Poetry." *Yale Review* 55 (1966): 255–64.

Buell, Lawrence. *Literary Transcendentalism.* Ithaca: Cornell University Press, 1975.

Cavell, Stanley. *The Senses of Walden.* New York: Viking, 1972.

Cook, Reginald. *Passage to Walden.* Boston: Houghton Mifflin, 1949.

Dillman, Richard H. "The Psychological Rhetoric of Walden." *ESQ; A Journal of the American Renaissance* 25 (1979): 79–91.

Fritzell, Peter A. "*Walden* and Paradox: Thoreau as Self-Conscious Ecologist." *New England Review and Bread Loaf Quarterly* 3 (1980): 51–67.

Garber, Frederick. *Thoreau's Redemptive Imagination.* New York: New York University Press, 1977.

Glick, Wendell. *The Recognition of Henry David Thoreau.* Ann Arbor: University of Michigan Press, 1970.

Gozzi, Raymond, ed. *Thoreau's Psychology: Eight Essays.* Lanham, Md.: University Press of America, 1983.

Gura, Philip F. "Henry Thoreau and the Wisdom of Words." *New England Quarterly* 52 (1979): 38–54.

———. "Language and Meaning: An American Tradition." *American Literature* 53 (1981): 1–21.

Harding, Walter. *The Days of Henry Thoreau.* New York: Knopf, 1966.

———. *Thoreau: A Century of Criticism.* Dallas: Southern Methodist University Press, 1954.

Hicks, John H. *Thoreau in Our Season.* Amherst: University of Massachusetts Press, 1966.

Hildebidle, John. *Thoreau: A Naturalist's Liberty.* Cambridge: Harvard University Press, 1983.

Howarth, William. *Thoreau's Life as a Writer.* New York: Viking, 1982.

Kellman, Steven G. "A Conspiracy Theory of Literature: Thoreau and You." *The Georgia Review* 32 (1978): 808–19.

Lebeaux, Richard. *Young Man Thoreau.* Amherst: University of Massachusetts Press, 1977.

Lewis, R. W. B. *The American Adam*. Chicago: University of Chicago Press, 1955.

Lyon, Melvin E. "Walden Pond as Symbol." *PMLA* 82 (1967): 289–300.

Matthiessen, F. O. *American Renaissance: Art and Expression in the Age of Emerson and Whitman*. New York: Oxford University Press, 1941.

McIntosh, James. *Thoreau as Romantic Naturalist*. Ithaca: Cornell University Press, 1974.

Meyer, Michael. *Several More Lives to Live: Thoreau's Political Reputation in America*. Westport, Conn: Greenwood, 1977.

———."Introduction." In *Walden and Civil Disobedience*, 7–36. Harmondsworth, Eng.: Penguin, 1983.

Michaels, Walter Benn. "*Walden*'s False Bottoms." *Glyph* no. 4 (1977): 132–46.

Moller, Mary Elkins. *Thoreau in the Human Community*. Amherst: University of Massachusetts Press, 1980.

Nash, Roderick. "Henry David Thoreau: Philosopher." In *Wilderness and the American Mind*, 84–95. New Haven: Yale University Press, 1982.

Neufeldt, Leonard N. "Henry David Thoreau's Political Economy." *New England Quarterly* 57 (1984): 359–82.

Paul, Sherman. *The Shores of America: Thoreau's Inward Exploration*. Urbana: University of Illinois Press, 1958.

———, ed. *Thoreau: A Collection of Critical Essays*. Englewood Cliffs, N.J.: Prentice-Hall, 1962.

Porte, Joel. *Emerson and Thoreau: Transcendentalists in Conflict*. Middletown, Conn.: Wesleyan University Press, 1966.

Rowe, John Carlos. " 'The Being of Language: The Language of Being' in *A Week on the Concord and Merrimack Rivers*." *boundary 2* 7, no. 3 (1979): 91–115.

Ruland, Richard, ed. *Twentieth-Century Interpretations of Walden*. Englewood Cliffs, N. J.: Prentice-Hall, 1968.

Seybold, Ethel. *Thoreau: The Quest and the Classics*. New Haven: Yale University Press, 1951.

Shanley, J. Lyndon. *The Making of Walden*. Chicago: University of Chicago Press, 1957.

Simon, Myron. "Thoreau and Anarchism." *Michigan Quarterly Review* 23 (1984): 360–84.

Smith, Herbert. "Thoreau among the Classical Economists." *ESQ; A Journal of the American Renaissance* 23 (1977): 114–22.

Stoller, Leo. *After Walden: Thoreau's Changing Views on Economic Man*. Palo Alto: Stanford University Press, 1957.

Sundquist, Eric. *Home as Found: Authority and Genealogy in Nineteenth-Century American Literature*. Baltimore: The Johns Hopkins University Press, 1979.

Taylor, Carole Anne. "Authorship without Authority: *Walden*, Kierkegaard, and the Experiment in Points of View." In *Kierkegaard and Literature: Irony, Repetition, and Criticism*, edited by Ronald Schliefer, et al., 168–82. Norman: University of Oklahoma Press, 1984.

Thoreau Quarterly (formerly the *Thoreau Journal Quarterly*). 1968–.

Van Doren, Mark. *Henry David Thoreau: A Critical Study*. New York: Russell & Russell, 1961.

Wagenknecht, Edward. *Henry David Thoreau: What Manner of Man?* Amherst: University of Massachusetts Press, 1981.

Walcutt, Charles Child. "*Walden* as a Response to 'The American Scholar.' " *Arizona Quarterly* 34 (1978): 5–30.

West, Michael. "Scatology and Escatology: The Heroic Dimensions of Thoreau's Wordplay." *PMLA* 89 (1974): 1043–64.

———. "Thoreau and the Language Theories of the French Enlightenment." *ELH* 51 (1984): 747–70.

Whitaker, Rosemary. "*A Week* and *Walden:* The River vs. the Pond" *The American Transcendental Quarterly* 17 (1973): 9–13.

Acknowledgments

"*Walden*: Thoreau's Unfinished Business" by Loren Eiseley from *The Star Thrower* by Loren Eiseley, © 1978 by the Estate of Loren C. Eiseley, Mabel L. Eiseley, Executrix. Reprinted by permission of Times Books, a Division of Random House, Inc.

"Part of a Winter" by George Sibley from *Mountain Gazette* no. 41 (January 1976), © 1976 by George Sibley. Reprinted by permission.

"Economic Metaphor Redefined: The Transcendental Capitalist at Walden" by Judith P. Saunders from *American Transcendental Quarterly* 36 (Fall 1977), © 1977 by Kenneth Walter Cameron. Reprinted by permission of Kenneth Walter Cameron.

" 'A True Integrity Day by Day': Thoreau's Organic Economy in *Walden*" by Harold Hellenbrand from *ESQ: A Journal of the American Renaissance* 25, no. 2 (1979), © 1979 by Harold Hellenbrand. Reprinted by permission.

"Private Discourse in Thoreau's *Walden*" by Ronald B. Schwartz from *The South Carolina Review* 13, no. 1 (Fall 1980), © 1980 by Clemson University. Reprinted by permission of *The South Carolina Review*.

"Houses and Compost: Thoreau's *Walden*" (originally entitled "Originality and Authority in Emerson and Thoreau") by Joseph G. Kronick from *American Poetics of History: From Emerson to the Moderns* by Joseph G. Kronick, © 1984 by Louisiana State University Press. Reprinted by permission.

"*Walden* and the 'Curse of Trade' " by Michael T. Gilmore from *American Romanticism and the Marketplace* by Michael T. Gilmore, © 1985 by the University of Chicago. Reprinted by permission of the University of Chicago Press.

"Thoreau's Dawn and the Lake School's Night" by Robert Weisbuch from *American Literature and British Influence in the Age of Emerson* by Robert Weisbuch, © 1986 by the University of Chicago. Reprinted by permission of the University of Chicago Press.

Index

of, 4, 5, 22–24, 36–38, 39,
114–15; earliness, search for by,
95, 96, 117–34; on easting meat,
73; as educator-legislator, 108–16;
rejection of Emerson by, 7–10,
11, 97; as extremist, 6–7; as first
person, 117; as good businessman,
63–64; health concerns of, 71;
houses, objection to, 90; history,
rejection of, 101, 109–10, 114,
115; incomplete vision of, 36–38;
on Irishmen, 34, 35–36; lack of
ambition of, 7; on the Lake
School, 126; Lake School poets,
influence of on, 117–34; life in
Concord of, 21–22, on life, 34,
38, 39, 117; as mental traveler, 18,
20; on modern man, 15; move to
Walden of, 33–34; narcissism of,
3–4; on old people, 117; on
ownership, 106; paradoxical
nature of, 16, 59; on philosophy,
20; as poet, 2; on politics, 74;
public reaction to, 50–51; on
reading, 8–9, 91; on redemption,
44; as realist, 6–7; rejection of
England by, 120–21, 133–34;
rejection of translations by, 92; as
rhetorician, 45–46; as romantic,
123; search for meaning of, 13–26;
self-awareness of, 5, 27; on self-
sufficiency, 106; on simplification,
35–36; on social reality, 105–6; on
speech, 93; on spirituality, 73–74;
as spiritual wanderer, 14; on
studying, 111; unrealistic
viewpoint of, 36–58; as walker,
128–29; Wordsworth's influence
on, 126–34; on writing, 92–93,
108–9. *Works: Cape Cod,* 23–24;
"Divinity School Address," 9;
journal, 17, 19, 22, 128; "Life
without Principle," 1; *The Maine
Woods,* 118, 120; "The Poets'
Delay," 126. *See also* "Civil
Disobedience"; *Walden; individual
chapters*
Thought, commodification of, 107,
110, 111–13
Time: economic imagery and, 62;
space and, 94–95, 96;

transcendental, 94–95; undoing of,
133; writing and, 96
"Tintern Abbey" (Wordsworth), 128,
129
Tocqueville, Alexis de, 111
Todd, John, 77
Transcendentalism, 10–11, 94–95
Tropes, 97

Understanding, subversion of, 81–82

Vegetarianism, symbol of, 73–74, 77
Vision, 125

Walden: as an account of success, 129;
boring quality of, 79; capitalism,
effect on, 114–16; capitalism in,
59–67; Coleridge's influence on,
121–26; conclusion of, 10, 101,
109, 114, 115; as defeated text,
101; delicateness of, 80; difficulty
of, for readers, 115; Emerson's
influence on, 8–11; history, denial
of, 109–10; language, paradoxical
use of, 62–67; literal vs.
metaphorical in, 80; mythic
quality of, 109–10; New Criticism
and, 2–3; New Testament and,
64–67, 69–70; paradox in, 16, 59,
62–67, 102, 110; as political tract,
107–8; private discourse in, 79–87;
religious imagery in, 60; revisions
of, 114–16; self-consciousness in,
8, 109–11; spontaneity of, 124;
time in, 133; as unfinished
business, 13–26; Wordsworth's
influence on, 126–34
Walden Pond, description of, 84–85
Walden's Dirty Language (West), 96
"*Walden's* False Bottoms" (Michaels),
89
Warren, Robert Penn, 2
*Week on the Concord and Merrimack
Rivers, A,* 95, 114, 115–16
West, Michael, 71, 75, 96
"Where I Lived and What I Lived
For," 81, 124
Whitehead, Alfred North, 18
Whiter, Walter, 96